Wicked
PHENIX CITY

Wicked PHENIX CITY

FAITH SERAFIN

Charleston · London

THE
History
PRESS

Published by The History Press
Charleston, SC 29403
www.historypress.net

Images are courtesy of the author unless otherwise noted.

First published 2014

Manufactured in the United States

ISBN 978.1.62619.543.1

Library of Congress CIP data applied for.

For my partner in crime, Christie Duell,

and

my cellmate, Cassie Clark.

CONTENTS

CONTENTS

ACKNOWLEDGEMENTS

L et me thank you, the reader, for taking the time to look into *Wicked Phenix City*. The support of my audiences, friends and family has been a great source of encouragement while taking on the challenge of a new series. Switching gears from my regular haunted history genre was an easy transition and a welcomed change, and I greatly appreciate the positivity and optimism from everyone who encouraged me while writing this book.

I would like to give a great deal of thanks to some members of the Muscogee Nation (Creek tribes of Oklahoma). I was privileged to have the opportunity to interview Mr. Jim Sanders of the White Bird Clan. At eighty-two years old, his knowledge of the history of his ancestors from the Coweta towns is remarkable. His family legacies have been passed down through generations by the same verbal traditions his ancestors used for thousands of years. Certainly, one of my most memorable experiences from this writing endeavor will be of sitting in Jim Sanders's tent, listening to him tell me the story of his people. I would also like to recognize Mr. Lee Littlehawk, descendant of the Tuckabatchee towns, for allowing me to photograph him in the traditional tribal clothing of the Muscogee people for the Native American–related chapters of this book. His input on the historical elements are also appreciated.

Lastly, I would like to thank Jeremy Dunman of Leader2 Photography for his help and knowledge regarding photo editing and all my colleagues and fellow writers who share an old (and new) love for the history of the American South.

Jim Sanders (age eighty-two) is descendant of the new or little Coweta Muscogee Indians. His ancestors can be traced back within the tribal town to the year 1300. His grandfather was known as the medicine man of Ochi. Jim lives in Oklahoma today and is proud of his legacies and the traditions of storytelling, still practiced by his people today.

INTRODUCTION

The Reverend Francis Lafayette Cherry wrote, "The greatest and most useful men, whose history is worth preserving, sprang mostly from the humble and obscure walks of life." This statement, from one of Russell and Lee County's earliest history books, is a testament to the people who have lived in the region that is today Phenix City, Alabama. The once turbulent and violent frontier times are hidden in the shadow of the 1950s, when it became known nationally as "Sin City." This era sprang from syndicated groups of gangsters, political corruption, illegal whiskey, gambling and prostitution. However, in the earliest history of what has been called "America's Wickedest City," there exists a platform of treason, murder, frontier justice and vice that conceived a location notorious for criminal activity.

Starting in the early 1800s, the vast populations of Muscogee Indians who lived in the primitive territories were the first recorded victims of European crimes. Though these ancient people had their own laws and customs for ill behavior and rule breaking, the clash of authorities and what was considered "savage" was scarcely different among the people who lived there. European encroachment led to raids, retaliations and ruthless executions by both settlers and natives who shared the Alabama frontier. This brutal battle for existence essentially crumbled the Indian empire and ultimately damaged the region for more than a century.

By 1900, the settlement of Girard, located on the banks of the Chattahoochee River, was known as an outlaw hideout and place of vice. Brewing and distilling spirits came with immigrants who settled in the lawless village, nicknamed "Sodom," and many of them found revenue in manufacturing and selling whiskey. Capitalizing on the manufacturing and distribution of alcohol, when the iron fist of Prohibition hit Alabama, Phenix City openly defied the laws and continued to make, sell and supply alcohol to cities all over the United States and abroad.

By the 1950s, Sin City had reached an era that was so corrupt that the city nearly destroyed itself. Generations of outlaws, illegal activity and malfeasance plummeted the city into near ruin, leading up to one of only a few cases of martial law to exist in America since the days of the Civil War.

The mythical bird for which Phenix City is named is a symbol of the city's very existence today. Legend says that the phoenix, a symbol of the sun, resurrection and rebirth, is destroyed by fire and reborn from the ashes. Phenix City, Alabama, has suffered years of hardships and crime, but it has been destroyed and risen from the ashes time and time again. From the frontier days of the American holocaust to establishing an outlaw town on the backs of criminals and vice, Phenix City is an ideal example of what doesn't kill us makes us stronger.

I

BAD BLOOD AND INDIAN WARS

Fort Mitchell Dueling Grounds

Fort Mitchell was established in 1812 by Commander John Floyd of the Georgia militia and was named for the Georgia governor David B. Mitchell. Its purpose was to protect the allied Creek towns in the Indian territories, and it was an encampment for militia soldiers. Because of its location on the old Indian trail between Augusta, Georgia, and St. Stephens, Alabama, soldiers could help settlers cross the unpredictable native territories in relative safety. In 1817, the trading post that was located at Fort Hawkins, in Macon, Georgia, moved to Fort Mitchell. Colonel John Crowell came to the fort in 1821 and helped bring order by serving as an Indian agent over the region's Creek territories.

Colonel Crowell and his brothers ran a tavern at the fort that entertained the last serving general in the Revolutionary War, the Marquis de Lafayette. He arrived at Fort Mitchell in March 1825 to tour the wild frontier of Alabama. Francis Scott Key, writer of the lyrics to "The Star-Spangled Banner," also stayed at the fort, as did President Andrew Jackson, General Thomas Jesup and General Winfield Scott during the second Creek War. Fort Mitchell was occupied by the United States Fourth Infantry Division from 1825 until 1840, and the location was also one of the starting points for the infamous Trail of Tears during the Indian removal. However, before the Indians were relocated and the fort abandoned, this neutral location served another purpose—a brutal

Fort Mitchell was named after Georgia governor David B. Mitchell, who
served from 1766 to 1837. *Courtesy of the Library of Congress.*

and savage one. It was the location used by many men, some of very
prominent social stature, to settle differences by dueling, most often to
the death.

The origins of dueling cannot be traced back to one particular source or
culture. History tells us that it is among one of the oldest means of settling
quarrels. Early accounts of duels from medieval times tell of brutal slayings
with crude weaponry, often leaving the loser to die a most agonizing death.
Over the centuries, rules and guidelines for dueling, including timed rounds
and medical treatment, helped evolve the gruesome bout into a fair but brutal
means of combat. The logic behind this primitive means of justice was to

give both parties the opportunity to defend their honor without involving vendettas between families.

The ancient Norse would meet at a designated location, dressed in full battle attire and carrying many different types of weapons that included broad axes, long swords and the deadly flail (a large iron or brass ball with sharp spikes fixed to a baton with a sturdy chain). Duels could be fought over ownership of property, debts or slander or to defend a friend or relative's honor. Some were "legally sanctioned" and were ordered when a resolution could not be found between parties. In these ancient Germanic tribes, if a challenge was set forth and the accused did not show, he would be ostracized and labeled *Niðingr*, which means "loss of honor."

In medieval Italy, Fiore dei Liberi, a fourteenth-century knight and fencing master, constructed a manual dedicated to the art of dueling known as the *Flower of Battle*. It is among the earliest known martial arts manuscripts and includes instructions on the use of swords and hand-to-hand combat. In the eighteenth century, the Irish Code Duello adopted the use of dueling pistols. Dueling pistols were made for the sole intent of killing. They were often more accurate and reliable than standard or military firearms. The Irish code of dueling with pistols is also one of the most recognized methods of dueling in the southern United States. Typically, rules were set forth, and witnesses gathered to attest to the fairness and circumstances of the duel. The rules of engagement were simple. Each challenger stood a designated distance away from the other, a signal was given and the opponents each fired one shot. If neither challenger was hit, they both reloaded their pistols and, upon the signal, fired again. On the third round, if one of the opponents was not dead or wounded, hand-to-hand combat or fencing could follow. Gun duels rarely escalated to the latter, and after the first or second shot, one challenger was typically mortally wounded or dead.

George Crawford and Thomas Burnside: Duel of 1828

At Fort Mitchell, located on the outskirts of Phenix City, are the remains of a frontier courtroom. The dueling grounds here have been soaked in the blood of both the innocent and the guilty and by the same means of primitive justice carried out by America's ancestors for thousands of years. A single marker now stands in the location where one of Fort Mitchell's most infamous duels took place.

The circumstances that led up to the duel of George Crawford and Thomas Burnside on the morning of January 5, 1828, were tragic—mostly because the two men were previously friends and also rising political figures in Georgia. The Crawford family was among Georgia's earliest and most prominent. Peter Crawford (George's father) was an attorney and veteran of the American Revolution. He established the family's stature by supporting and contributing to Georgia's political factions. George also had a cousin, William, who was a leading politician in Columbia County and held two presidential bids, running in 1816 and 1824.

George followed in his father and uncle's footsteps, attending Princeton and studying law. He was admitted to the state bar in 1822 and served as a second lieutenant for the Georgia state militia from 1824 to 1825. He later joined the ranks of politicians in Georgia in 1827. He was also appointed to succeed Thomas Wells, Georgia attorney general, that same year. During this time, a letter was submitted to newspapers in Augusta, Georgia, criticizing Peter Crawford and his family, who dominated the political factions. The letter was allegedly written by a woman who, to this day, remains unknown. Crawford confronted the editors of the papers, but they refused to tell him who the female writer was. He continued his demands, and eventually his friend and colleague Congressman Thomas Burnside stepped up to defend the nameless woman and uphold her anonymity. This resulted in flaring tempers between the friends, escalating to heated arguments and repeated attacks of character and honor.

Essentially, the continuous quarrelling resulted in the challenge of a duel. Crawford would defend his family name, and Burnside would not allow his merits in defending a woman to be denied. The State of Georgia had not yet outlawed dueling, but there were severe repercussions for political figures involved in acts of violence. Arrangements had to be made for the two men to meet outside the state. In the event that one of the men was killed, the other could face murder charges, so to avoid the extradition laws of Georgia, it was necessary to hold the duel in a neutral location. At the time, Fort Mitchell was independent from the state of Alabama and was still part of the Indian Territory, so Crawford and Burnside agreed to hold the duel there in order to avoid the consequences of state laws.

Thomas Burnside and George Crawford left their homes near Augusta, Georgia, for Fort Mitchell in December 1827. While en route, they met at an inn and spoke cordially for the remainder of the trip. Their demeanor was not combative in the least; in fact, their traveling companions were confident that they would resolve their differences and cancel the duel. Thomas

Burnside was not so optimistic, and on the night before the event was to take place, he wrote a letter to his wife, Catherine. It read:

> *Dear Wife and Mother:*
> *Tomorrow I fight. I do it on Principle. Whatever be my fate. I believe I am right. On this ground I have acted and will act. I believe I shall succeed, but if I do not I am prepared for the consequences. Kiss the children and tell them that if I fall my last thought was of them.*
>
> *Yours most affectionately,*
> *Thomas Burnside*

On the morning of January 5, 1828, the cold, still air hung over the old Indian fort like a cloud of impending doom. An icy frost blanketed the ground, and the sun hid behind a cloudy and desolate sky. A small crowd of soldiers, including Colonel Crowell, and a few Indians gathered at the fort to watch the engagement unfold. The rules were set, and both men loaded their pistols accordingly. The signal was given to fire, and George Crawford and Thomas Burnside both lowered the hammers on their sidearms. Tom's shot met the ground just inches from George, covering him in ice and dirt. Tom politely apologized as he reloaded his pistol. A friend of his, who had recently survived a duel, stepped forward and announced that if he would apologize to George, his opponent would accept, and they could both leave unharmed. Tom shook his head and denied his friend's request. On the signal of the second round, both men fired. Again, neither of the men was hit, and they began to reload for the last round. Tom's friend must have sensed that this would be his final opportunity to ask him to apologize. He interjected his pleas more earnestly this time, but again, they fell on deaf ears. The final signal was given, shots rang out across the field and the smoke from the black powder pistols smothered the bystanders. Before the smoke lifted, a gasp came from Thomas Burnside. He exhaled his final breath and fell backward into the arms of his friend who had been desperately trying to avoid this outcome. Thomas Burnside was dead.

Because of the distance (six or seven days) from Augusta, Georgia, Tom's body had to be buried at Fort Mitchell. He was laid to rest, and word of his death was dispatched to his family. Two weeks later, the news reached his wife. She collapsed in despair and nearly died herself from shock. She later moved her family to Dahlonega, Georgia, with the hopes that a fresh start would help her cope with the loss of her husband. Because of the terrible victory, obtained through such a tragic event, George Crawford made

Thomas Burnside was buried at Fort Mitchell Cemetery on January 5, 1828, after he was killed in a duel by his rival, George W. Crawford.

substantial financial contributions to the Burnside family for many years. Those contributions were delivered to the Burnside family from "a friend of Tom's."

George Crawford went on to become governor of Georgia in 1843. In 1849, he was appointed secretary of war under President Zachary Taylor. He is also considered the author of Georgia's Ordinance of Secession, which was written in 1861. He carried with him, his whole life, the heavy heart and burden of killing his friend and colleague Thomas Burnside. George Crawford died at his family's Belair Estate near Augusta on July 27, 1872. The Crawford-Burnside duel of 1828 sparked much controversy over the involvement of political figures in duels. Subsequently, this resulted in a state law that prevented those involved in duels from holding polictical or government offices in Georgia. George Crawford went to his grave calling the duel between Tom and himself "a deplorable and unfortunate affair."

General Sowell Woolfolk and Joseph Camp: Duel of 1831

General Sowell Woolfolk and Joseph Camp were also among the political men who dueled at Fort Mitchell. The feud that led up to this event most likely stemmed from a long political dispute and also had roots in the factions of Georgia's government, similar to those that caused the duel between Crawford and Burnside. There are other stories surrounding the mystery that add to the confusion over why the feud took place at all. Those stories also suggest that there was likely some war mongering and provoking by both men's colleagues.

Some of the earliest accounts of trouble involving Sowell Woolfolk were documented in an article in the *Augusta Chronicle* in March 1827. Thomas Triplett was a sub-Indian agent for the Creek territory and was disgruntled over the fact that Woolfolk had rented out property without his consent. Thomas Triplett and his brother, Hillary, gathered a gang of white men, African American slaves and Indians to attack Woolfolk's properties. The gang of men burned down seven buildings belonging to Woolfolk, and when they caught up to him, they pointed their rifles and guns and threatened to kill Woolfolk on the spot.

General Woolfolk escaped the ordeal, but about a year later, more trouble followed when Hillary Triplett and Columbus, Georgia commissioner Philip Alston used Woolfolk as a mediator, sharing some combative correspondence in the *Columbus Ledger* over an issue they wanted to resolve with a duel. Correspondence printed in the *Columbus Ledger* on August 1828 read:

> *Columbus, June 15, 1828*
> *Mr. H. Triplett*
> *Sir—When I requested Mr. Williamson to call you for a fist fight, I gave no author, nor shall I now. I only purpose to you a fight. Cowards only ask for an author.*
> > *Yours & Co. Philip Alston*

> *Columbus, June 15, 1828*
> *Mr. Hillary Triplett*
> *Sir—Your conduct requires satisfaction. My friend, Col. Woolfolk, is authorized to make arrangements for me.*
> > *Yours Philip H. Alston*

Columbus, June 15, 1828
Col. Philip H. Alston
Sir—I accept your challenge of this date and so soon as I can command the services of my friend (say between the sixth and tenth of July) you shall hear from me.

Hillary Triplett

Three of Woolfolk's colleagues did attempt to mediate the situation, but to no avail. Hillary Triplett would agree to meet Alston only at a location known as "Polecat Springs." Woolfolk would not agree to the terms since the location gave Triplett an unfair advantage. It was known as a place of assassination. He denied Triplett's request, and eventually Alston submitted a letter stating that he had been misrepresented; the misunderstanding had contributed to the challenge, and he withdrew.

In 1831, Sowell Woolfolk and another Columbus man named Joseph Camp both served as city administrators. Woolfolk was the city's intendant, and Camp was an attorney and commissioner. Both men were political figures and were among the high social classes of the Columbus elite. The early details of the dispute between Woolfolk and Camp are unclear, but the long debate finally erupted into a bitter argument while both men were in Milledgeville, Georgia (the state capital at the time). Both of the men's colleagues instigated the feud, and with heavy provoking by local papers fueling the bitter rivalry, the men made plans to settle their differences over a duel at Fort Mitchell. Crawford and Burnside had met the night before, and it seemed that they had resolved the matter somewhat. An announcement was made that said the duel had been postponed, but the city would have its fight, and local papers stoked the cooling tempers between the two adversaries.

On January 23, 1931, in Columbus, Georgia, Sophie Woolfolk, Sowell Woolfolk's newlywed wife, and her family gathered in one of the Woolfolk waterfront buildings along the Chattahoochee River. It was located directly across from the Fort Mitchell dueling grounds. She watched anxiously as the men loaded their pistols and took position opposite each other on the field. The signal was given, and both men drew their pistols. Woolfolk fired first, and his round hit Camp right above the naval. The surgeon on hand described the wound as dangerous, but his colleagues, who had so eagerly been provoking and encouraging the duel, noted it was little more than a flesh wound. Camp then fired at Woolfolk and shot him just above the heart, most likely severing a major artery as the bullet passed completely through him. Blood gushed through his esophagus and out of his mouth as Woolfolk staggered for only a few seconds. As he looked down at the bullet wound in his chest, he muttered, "He has killed me." He then fell to the ground and died almost instantly. As Woolfolk's flag was hoisted at his demise, his poor wife collapsed and wept uncontrollably.

The following day, General Woolfolk was laid to rest at Linwood Cemetery in Columbus. A friend of Woolfolk named John Milton received the news that his friend had been killed, and he made it his personal mission to assassinate Camp over the matter. His vendetta was fueled by the unjustified means of his friend's death, and he traveled from Tennessee to Georgia to carry out the dreadful task. While Milton was en route to Columbus, he stopped at an inn in Franklin, Georgia, and spent the night. While there, he allegedly told a man about his plans to kill Joseph Camp.

The following day, in August 1833, Milton waited for Camp as he walked up the street near Howard's General Store in Columbus. Once he was within range, Milton unloaded both barrels of his shotgun into Camp, killing him right there on the sidewalk. Milton was arrested and charged with the assassination and murder of Joseph Camp. However, he was able to escape prosecution due to the friends Woolfolk had working with the judicial system in Columbus. The community of Columbus was sickened that John Milton "was not hanged for this act, cowardly as it was." Like all the men who died for honor at Fort Mitchell's dueling grounds, in the heart of the unjust, there beats a relenting vendetta that can be satisfied only with death.

The Treaty of Indian Springs and the Murder of Chief William McIntosh

The great Sioux chief Sitting Bull once said:

> *I am a redman. If the Great Spirit had desired me to be a white man, he would have made me so in the first place. He put in your heart certain wishes and plans, in my heart he put other and different desires. Each man is good in his sight. It is not necessary for Eagles to be Crows. We are poor…but we are free. No white man controls our footsteps. If we must die…we die defending our rights.*

These words ring true in almost all aspects of native treaties and in the demise of Indian culture all over the United States. Since the Clovis period, dating back to the ancient time of the Paleo-Indians, who lived in the southern regions of the United States, migration was essential for the tribes to maintain food and shelter. Over hundreds of years, these indigenous people formed family groups that evolved into tribes and towns. Each town had its own name, and the tribes had independent migratory patterns. Prehistoric bloodlines of mixed families expanded the lineage of these native people, and family units banded together with other tribes to form stronger groups in order to maintain their prosperity.

In the southern United States, the Muscogee people (also known as Creeks) evolved as a nation and maintained a relationship with their kinsman throughout the regions that are today Alabama, Georgia, Florida and Mississippi. They built homes and trading posts and organized councils to manage large populations of settlements. Chieftains and councils of men and women within the Muscogee tribes delegated the issues of economy, trade, law and everyday life in Indian towns. When hostilities broke out between neighboring tribes or invaders from France and Spain, the largest populations of tribes in the Alabama, Georgia and Florida regions established themselves as capital cities known as Coweta and Cusseta. Coweta was located near what is today Phenix City, on the Alabama side of the Chattahoochee River. Cusseta was located just north of Coweta, on the Georgia side of the river. Both towns were Creek but divided into different tribes, known as the Upper and Lower Creeks (which would later be known as the Red Sticks and White Sticks).

During the time that European settlers started to encroach on the Indian territories, land disputes became a regular issue. Some settlers came with legal deeds to property they acquired from the United States government. Others came as squatters. Squatters were people who had no legal claim to a property or land but settled it anyway, only to declare a right to it once they had established themselves for a certain amount of time. This is known as "squatter's rights."

In the time of the frontier South, most settlers lived among the native tribes in relative harmony. Many of the earliest families in Russell County married into the tribes and adopted their culture and means of living. Settlers and Indians living in one another's midst, particularly in the Lower Creek town of Coweta, were tolerant of their neighbors. However, with that advantage came a huge disadvantage for the American Indians—one that would cost them not only their homes and families but also their lands and essentially their lives. Tribes divided, and the government's appetite for Indian land eventually led to uprisings and feuds between natives and the settlers. During this time, settling in the Indian territories was dangerous and was considered to be the most formidable means of living there was.

In colonial times, when European explorers were coming to the New World, James Oglethorpe settled the colony of Savannah, Georgia.

James Oglethorpe was an English general and reformist. He brought prisoners from England's debtor's prisons to populate the Savannah colony in what is today Georgia. *Courtesy of the Library of Congress.*

Oglethorpe was a British general and also a reformist, seeking to remedy the terrible abuse that was taking place in debtor's prisons in England. He petitioned the British Parliament for permission to take prisoners and their families, who might otherwise end up impoverished in London, to the New World in order to build colonies and fight for the Royal Army. Many of those inmates were Scottish and Irish immigrants. Hundreds of them were released to Oglethorpe, and they fought for England against the imposing forces that sought to take over the colony of Georgia.

One of those Scottish soldiers was John McIntosh of Barlum, Scotland. His son William grew up at the Darien settlement, living and working among the Creek Indians who also lived in the coastal region. When William was only nineteen, he fought in the colonial army alongside the Creek warriors, defending the Georgia colony against the Spanish. William was promoted to captain and soon met the daughter of a Creek chief named Senoia Henneha. Senoia, Georgia, located in Coweta County, is named for the Indian princess, but little is actually known about her. She was part of the "Wind Clan," a prominent band of Muscogee Indians that was among the Creek elite and oldest in ancestral attributes. Her father was most likely a high-ranking chief in the Lower Creek towns. William also took another Creek wife a few years later, adopting polygamy, which was accepted and common in the native culture. He later moved south with his father and settled at McIntosh Bluffs, located near present-day Mobile, Alabama.

In the 1700s, the territory of Georgia stretched from the Atlantic Ocean to the Mississippi River, and the state of Alabama did not yet exist. This territory belonged to the Muscogee people and was home to William and Senoia. In 1775, Senoia gave birth to her son and named him after his father. William McIntosh was born near what is today Wetumpka, Alabama, and grew up learning from his Creek relatives, as well as his father's Scottish customes. He was bilingual and spoke fluent Muscogee but did not learn to write in English until adulthood. His father's military engagements also helped William understand his role in the colonial army, as well as trading in the frontier economy. William and his brother Roley were both considered Wind Clan royalty. They were taught to fish and hunt by their uncles. They also participated in the Indian festivals and religious ceremonies and understood the Muscogee people's desires to maintain their culture, their land and their heritage.

William McIntosh's father left for a period to fight in the Revolutionary War. Upon his return, he was eager to remain with his family but approached the Indian council of his wife's clan to ask them to allow William and Roley to accompany him overseas. With the war still at hand, and the growing encroachment of white settlers, it seemed necessary to give his children an education and learn European customs. However, the governing rules that dictated the boys within the tribe denied his request. A few years later, father William made the decision to leave his Indian family in the Lower Creek towns, and at that point his marriages were considered "broken" (meaning he was divorced). He settled near Mobile, in what is today Washington County, Alabama.

William remarried and built a new home. He often saw his sons when they came to visit. As they grew into men, the conversations between them and their father always seemed to reflect the pleasant existence shared by the Creeks and settlers. Their father told them stories of the colonial wars, when he witnessed his father, John, taken as prisoner by the Spanish. He spoke of the bravery he saw in the Indian warriors, stating, "They were as fierce as the Scots."

When William was nineteen, his father passed away. He left shortly after and returned to his home in Coweta with an inheritance of several horses. Because of his prominent status in the Wind Clan, he was quickly sent to the forefront of the tribe as a leader. He organized and led war parties against his hostile neighbors and defended his people as a warrior. He was later given the name *Taskanugi Hatke*, which means, "White Warrior."

At twenty five, William was chosen as a Coweta chief. Coweta was among the four oldest towns in the Creek nation. The others were Cusseta, Tuckabatchee and Osweechee. Because Cusseta was recognized as the oldest town in the Creek Nation, a claim that Coweta argued, tribal councils were held there. The Coweta territory spanned the distance between Broken Arrow, which is modern-day Phenix City, Alabama, to the Cherokee Territory, which is today the regions of north Alabama and Georgia. At that time, it was the largest native body in both size and population. With McIntosh's new role as *micco* (king or chief), he was granted an honor that placed him above all other chiefs in the nation due to his legacies in the Wind Clan. His superiority was unrivaled, but his responsibility was a heavy burden.

William married Eliza Grierson. Like William, her father was also a Scotsman and fur trader who settled among the Creeks and took a Creek woman as his wife. William and Eliza lived near the Tallapoosa River in what is today Carroll County, Georgia, and raised a family— two girls, Jane and Kate, and a son, Chilly. William raised his children

William McIntosh was born in 1775. His father was a Scottish fur trader from Barlum, Scotland, and his mother was a prominent member of the Muscogee Wind Clan. His mixed heritage gave him an advantage in his tribal community until the downfall of the Muscogee nation. He was later assassinated by his own people.

just as he was raised. They were bilingual and understood the cultures of their heritages.

For some time before William McIntosh was inducted as chief, fraudulent treaties and bad land deals between the United States government and Indian chiefs throughout the Creek territories and other Native American nations were becoming a serious problem. The impending loss of everything the natives held sacred—their lands, history and culture—was looming, with no regard for the people or their ancestral homes. Tribes divided themselves into peaceful and hostile sects, driving a wedge between the Creek Confederacy and creating chaos among the disagreeing chiefs and tribal towns. These issues led to many uprising, raids, murders, kidnappings and other unlawful acts by the Indians against the settlers.

As Coweta and the other Lower Creek towns strove to live in peace with their white neighbors, the Upper Creeks became increasingly hostile toward not only the whites but also their Creek kinsman. As tensions between the towns rose, settlers were as uncertain of the outcome as the Creeks were, and a resolution had to be found in order to regain order and peace among the frontier people.

Among the Seminole tribes of Florida (which were also part of the Creek Confederacy), the chief Little Prince rose to power after his predecessor, Alexander McGillivray, was released by his tribesmen for signing a treaty they felt was not trustworthy. Little Prince was an avid supporter of McIntosh, and the two became great associates and friends. During the same time, Tustennugee Thlucco, or "Big Warrior," who lived at Tuckabatchee, became chief of the Upper Creek towns, and the fearless chief Menawa, from Oakfuskee and the Hillabee villages, became the Upper Creek war chief.

Menewa was born of mixed race as well. His mother was a prominent Creek woman from the Upper Creek town of Oakfuskee, and his father was also a Scottish fur trader. His given name was *Hothlepoya*, which translates to "Crazy Trouble Hunter." He grew up through the maternal linage in his mother's clan, but he showed no affinity toward his father and did not even recognize his mixed heritage. He was later given the role of chief at Oakfuskee, and his name was then changed to *Menewa*, meaning "Great Warrior."

Menewa was suspicious of McIntosh and his popularity in the Creek towns. He knew that much of the governing body, being Coweta, favored the leadership of mixed Indians. This was because of their ability to delegate on behalf of their tribe and the United States government. The ability to remain

Chief Menewa was a mixed-race Muscogee war chief who fought on behalf of the Red Sticks. He was shot, stabbed and fought until he collapsed at the Battle of Horseshoe Bend in 1814. He barely survived the fight but continued to support the Indian holy wars led throughout the South by the legendary Shawnee chief Tecumseh.

neutral but maintain economic, religious and cultural balance seemed easier for those of mixed blood, and this was something other tribesmen were becoming increasingly concerned over. This gained McIntosh a terrible adversary in Menewa, and the struggles that started with suspicion would come full circle and essentially ruin both of them in the end.

The United States was still recovering from the American Revolution when treaties were established to expand farther west. In 1802, the treaty of Fort Wilkerson was signed, and the United States bought Georgia's claims to all territories from the Oconee River, near Milledgeville, Georgia, to the Mississippi River—almost the entire territory within the Creek nation. The growing hostilities were now evident among the encroached natives, and the Creek towns organized a council to discuss the issue of land treaties and the adversity they would face if they refused to sign over or sell their land.

President George Washington appointed Benjamin Hawkins as Indian agent over all the Indian territories south of the Ohio River. Hawkins wanted to implement a more civilized life among the native people, teaching them to farm and become laborers. He helped build schools like the Ashbury Mission, which was located near Fort Mitchell in Coweta, and he worked closely with the chiefs and sub-agents to maintain balance and communication.

During the time Thomas Jefferson served as president, he called for Hawkins to gather the chiefs of the Creek Nation to meet in Washington and discuss land near the Ocmulgee River. William McIntosh was chosen by Hawkins to act as an interpreter for the deliberation. On November 14, 1803, the Creek chiefs and Hawkins met with Secretary of War Henry Dearborn to discuss the purchase of more land. The proposed land near the Ocmulgee River was important to the Creeks. One of their most sacred ceremonial lodges and religious center were part of the location where the president wanted to clear a horse path for settlers traveling to Fort Stoddert (near Mobile) to ensure their safety. This was not reasonable to the chiefs, and they felt strongly that they had already made sufficient provisions to ensure the safety of settlers. They were very defiant and unmoved by Dearborn, who demanded they turn over the land.

The Creek tribes had already been forced to move toward the coast because of the growing white settlements. Coastal areas had fewer game and land, causing a shortage of food. Also, sicknesses that had not previously plagued the Indians came with the Europeans who sailed to the New World. McIntosh explained to Dearborn these concerns of the chiefs. He warned that allowing more settlers to travel and live on their land would lead to trouble. Dearborn quickly assured him that laws would be written to ensure the safety of both white settlers and Indians. But the pressure the government placed on the chiefs was too great, and the treaty was signed, giving the United States more than one-third of the Georgia claim.

In 1803, the United States purchased Louisiana from France in the controversial Louisiana Purchase. This pushed the options of new territory farther away from the natives as they helplessly watched the United States devour their home. England's defeat was a victorious milestone for America,

The ancient Indian city of Ocmulgee was a sacred location to the Muscogee people. It was a major center for commerce and religious ceremonies and had been continuously inhabited by humans for seventeen thousand years until 1836.

but President Thomas Jefferson was already working on plans for the removal of all Indians, starting with the Cherokees and Creeks who had fought against America under the royal Crown.

The new country was growing quickly, and a civil war between the native people was becoming imminent. On August 5, 1811, dressed in the traditional red-and-white feather headdress symbolizing peace to his fellow kinsman but war on the settlers, the Shawnee chief Tecumseh gathered twenty warriors and met at the new Creek capital, Tuckabatchee, for the National Council. He gave an elaborate speech, outlining his concerns over the encroachment of the settlers and the dwindling land of the Indians. He was calling on his native kinsman to support a holy war against all European settlers and to destroy the United States government. McIntosh's concern grew as the crowds of warriors and chiefs roared with approval. They were undoubtedly swayed by the emotional and fiery speech of the old warrior. The Creek Nation was to have its rebellion.

The National Council was active for almost a week. McIntosh, Big Warrior, Little Prince and Menewa all spoke with Tecumseh but would not commit to his rebellion. Later, McIntosh reported the actions of the

Lee Littlehawk is a Muscogee descendant of the Tuckabatchee village. Tuckabatchee was one of the former capitals of the Creek nation and home to the legendary chief Big Warrior.

council to the Indian agent, Benjamin Hawkins. Hawkins didn't see the suggestion of rebellion as a threat and disregarded the concern that McIntosh felt was substantial. McIntosh was torn; part of him wanted to join the rebellion and fight to return the Indians to peace and the old ways, but another part of him knew that the United States was too powerful a force to fight against and win.

Without duress, in 1812, murders and raids became a far too common occurrence in the Indian territories. Reports of entire families being butchered by war-mongering Creeks were terrorizing the southern frontier. At the expense of the murdered frontier people, Hawkins finally started to take the

Tecumseh was a Shawnee chief and warrior who led a holy war against European settlers and the United States government. He was killed at the Battle of Thames in 1813. After his death, the Indian nations quickly dissolved, and the fighting ended.

threat of rebellion seriously. He had McIntosh gather his council to meet and discuss what could be done to stop the crimes against the settlers. McIntosh was ordered to lead a war party to find the renegade killers and administer justice according to Indian laws—in other words, kill them.

Six culprits were captured by McIntosh's party and were shot and killed without question. Others who were involved were tortured and whipped in an effort to teach them a lesson and to let the opposing Creek tribes know this kind of behavior would not be tolerated. But it did not have the effect for which they hoped.

At the same time, a war party among the Upper Creeks was also being organized to lead the rebellion against settlers and anyone who supported the United States, including their kinsmen. Retaliations broke out on both sides of the Muscogee tribes, and many were killed in the growing anger and confusion of what Tecumseh called his "holy war." Tecumseh's leaders, Joseph Francis (who was also a tribe prophet), High-Head Jim and Peter McQueen, led the rebellion and received weapons from the Spaniards in Pensacola to support their cause. The Upper Creeks were now known as the "Red Sticks." Red signified the color of war. They painted their faces bright red, along with their war clubs and clothing.

The Upper and Lower Creeks were now divided and engaged in a civil war to regain their rights through force. The Red Sticks attacked Fort Mims on August 30, 1813. Conveniently, the gate was left unlocked by a drunken major who was killed in the attack. This costly mistake led to the massacre of over five hundred men, women and children; friendly Creeks; and several Spanish and black prisoners.

News of the attacks reached Washington, and orders came down to the Georgia militia to respond with force. Hawkins dispatched McIntosh under military orders and promoted him to the rank of major. McIntosh immediately organized a war party to aid the United States, which he did without question. Also commissioned with McIntosh was Timpoochee Barnard, who was also a mixed-race Lower Creek chief from the tribe located on the border of the Cusseta town. General John Floyd of the Georgia militia, General John White of the East and Middle Tennessee Divisions and Brigadier General Andrew Jackson of the Second Division all gathered their forces to respond to the massacre at Fort Mims. Andrew Jackson also raised an army of volunteers that included different tribes from all over the South. Among them were Creeks, Choctaws, Chickasaws and Cherokees, who came from as far north as Tennessee and as far west as Mississippi to fight for the United States against the Red Stick army.

According to several historical accounts, the gates at Fort Mims were accidently left unlocked by a drunken major. This careless mistake led to the murder of over five hundred men, women and children; friendly Creeks; and Spanish and black prisoners.

General Jackson established Fort Deposit at the southern point of the Tennessee River. Under his command, he ordered General John Coffee of the Georgia militia to attack the Upper Creek settlement of Tallahatche, just a few miles from Ten Islands (modern-day Gadsden, Alabama), where the Red Sticks stood fast. General Coffee burned the town to the ground, took 84 prisoners and killed 184 Red Stick warriors. Equal to Jackson was General John Cocke. He had an unrelenting tendency to disregard correspondence from Jackson and ignore his requests for help or council. One of General Cocke's commanding officers, James White, received word from Cocke to attack the Hillabee Villages. Cocke's failure to correspond with Jackson left him unaware that at the time he sent orders for White to attack the village, Jackson was already negotiating its surrender. This particular town was the home of the Creek war chief Menewa. When Cocke's unit attacked the village, the natives were caught completely off guard. This infuriated Menewa and his warriors, and they vowed to join the allegiances of the Red Sticks.

Major McIntosh and Major Barnard arrived at the sacred war grounds of Autassee (present-day Shorter, Alabama) on November 29, 1813. The

General Andrew Jackson began his military career on the Tennessee frontier. He successfully defeated the Indian forces during the American Indian Wars and also defeated the British at the Battle of New Orleans. He later became America's seventh president. *Courtesy of the Library of Congress.*

original order from General John Floyd was for McIntosh and his men to cut off the escape of the Red Stick army on the west side of the Tallapoosa River. Because of cold temperatures and high water, McIntosh and his men were forced to relocate and, instead, cut off the northern escape route of the Red Sticks.

Floyd's unit was spotted by a Red Stick scout, and they quickly evacuated their camp. However, when the remaining forces opened fire on Floyd's unit, the few Red Stick warriors who remained were easily subdued by the heavy artillery. When the smoke started to settle on the battlefield, McIntosh and Barnard could see from their position that the Red Sticks were gaining an advantage under the smoke cover, and they moved their men into position to counterattack the imposing forces before they could inflict damage to Floyd's unit.

Floyd spoke highly of the courageous and selfless acts by McIntosh and Barnard and how their strategy and keen sense of battle helped gain the victory at Autassee. William McIntosh was quickly learning the military tactics used by the United States Army, and he was eager to support the cause in order to bring peace back to his home. General Andrew Jackson led his army to Tallaspoosa, where he defeated more than five hundred of the Red Sticks, and then to Enotochocpo, where his men, under extreme duress from scarce supplies and food shortages, were pushed back and forced to retreat to Fort Strother, which was located in what is today Saint Clair County, Alabama.

On March 24, 1814, Jackson regrouped his forces and set out for the Red Stick stronghold at Tohopeka. This battle is also known as Horseshoe Bend. Here, on March 27, the greatest power of the Red Stick army made their final stand against "Old Hickory." Under the command of the war chief Menawa, the Red Sticks would engage in the deadliest battle of the Indian Wars. Just before dawn, Jackson ordered his men to attack the Red Stick encampment that had been fortified with a log wall barrier between Jackson's army and the village. As Jackson's men settled into position around the Indian fortress, so did General Coffee's Indian forces in the surrounding woods. A team of Indian spies also took positions behind trees to aid as sharpshooters, and Major McIntosh's and Major Barnard's Creek warriors supported them as infantry. A number of Cherokees also accompanied the effort, including George Sequoyah Guess (creator of the first written alphabet of the Cherokee language).

Fighting commenced as General Jackson fired three- and six-pound cannons at the log barrier for nearly two hours. The infantry under his command grew closer and closer to the log barrier. Finally, without orders, a few warriors eager to go into battle jumped into the river and swam to the canoes intended for the Red Sticks' getaway. This would instigate the fighting, and it grew increasingly. As the queer mixture of uniformed soldiers and half-naked warriors converged onto the wall, the red-painted faces of the fierce Red Sticks began to emerge. Howling war cries and shrieks of agony could be heard among the gun and cannon fire. The battle was almost timeless, as it raged for hours. Major Lemuel Montgomery, for whom the capital city of Alabama is named, jumped onto the log wall and yelled for his fellow infantrymen to follow him. He was shot in the head and killed instantly.

Soldiers under the command of General Andrew Jackson attacked the Indian settlements at Horseshoe Bend on March 27, 1814. The most intense battle of the Indian wars occurred here and took the lives of over 850 men and wounded more than 200.

Major McIntosh led his men across the river and engaged the enemy. Most of Jackson's men had already broken the log barrier and were inside the Red Stick fortification. The spiritual advisor, who was appointed by Tecumseh to aid Menawa, gave an unauthorized order to pull the warriors back from the wall. Outraged by the audacity to give such an order in the middle of battle, the hot-headed Menawa killed the advisor and ordered his men back to the wall. He then jumped into the fight himself and fought through the onslaught of gunfire, stabbing swords, sabers, tomahawks, arrows, hand-to-hand combat and all the other gruesome tools and brutalities of battle.

The old warrior fought with amazing agility, strength and endurance but finally collapsed in exhaustion. Menawa had been stabbed repeatedly, shot seven times and was left for dead. After the fighting stopped, he woke up and slowly raised himself to see if he was among any other survivors. He saw the White Stick warriors combing over the battlefield, prodding the dead for signs of life. He noticed that they were not checking the dead women and children who had been slain when Jackson's men butchered the nearby village of Tohopeka. He crawled along the ground some fifteen feet away, covered himself in the blood-soaked dress of an Indian woman and again fell unconscious. As Menawa regained consciousness, he made the mistake of reaching up and grabbed the leg of a warrior who was just passing by, believing he was a dead squaw. When he grabbed the warrior, the man drew his rifle and fired at Menawa, ripping apart the flesh from his face and several of his teeth. The warrior then left Menawa, believing he was dead. Stunned but very much alive, Menawa waited until night. He crawled to the safety of the river and escaped in one of the remaining canoes left by Jackson's army.

After Jackson's victory at Horseshoe Bend, he was offered the position of brigadier general and accepted. He then took it upon himself, without the consent of Agent Hawkins, to negotiate a treaty at Fort Toulouse (also known as Fort Jackson, located in present-day Wetumpka, Alabama), demanding the surrender of Creek territory that included the Lower Creek towns. This was an unexpected slap in the face for the Creeks who had fought and died under Jackson's command against the Red Sticks. Now, not only were the loyal White Sticks fighting a civil war against their kinsmen, but they were also being forced by their commander to surrender their own lands.

This infuriated the Lower Creek chiefs, and tempers flared as they exchanged heated debates over the unfairness of the treaty. Essentially, the White Stick chiefs were forced to sign the treaty of Fort Toulouse, and the remaining Creek warriors were mustered out of the United States Army. McIntosh returned to his home in Coweta and took two more wives, who were from Cherokee tribes. He enrolled his eldest children in the Milledgeville Academy to further their educations, and he worked quietly on his plantation located on the Chattahoochee River. His life now reflected what he had worked so hard to achieve: peace and tranquility. The same could not be said for the broken tribesmen of the Creek towns that were left destitute and poor. Entire villages had been destroyed, and the people were scattered throughout the territory with nowhere to go.

The Red Sticks made another attempt to raise the rebellion when they sided with the British, who had permission to land in Spanish territory in order to train a combat team of black marines made up of runaway slaves and Red Stick warriors. McIntosh was informed and dispatched the information to Hawkins, who then relayed the message and received word to dispatch McIntosh and his men to respond to the threat. McIntosh's longtime supporter, Big Warrior of Tuckabatchee, pleaded with him to consider siding with the Red Sticks and the British. McIntosh would not be swayed; he felt he was doing the right thing by standing by his initial decision to fight for the United States. His fellow chieftains were not as optimistic,

After the Red Stick army was defeated, England made another attempt to raise the rebellion. The Spanish were contracted by British governors to land their ships and train battalions of black marines. Pictured here is a junior ROTC group from New Orleans, Louisiana, taken at the bicentennial event at Horseshoe Bend, 2014.

and many dropped their support of McIntosh, believing him to be a traitor and charlatan.

McIntosh was promoted to brigadier general in 1817 and fought under the command of General Andrew Jackson to control the hostilities of the remaining Red Sticks until 1819, when he was again discharged from the army. He had hunted down the remaining Red Stick enemies and dealt with them according to Indian laws. All except for one: Menawa.

When McIntosh returned home from nearly six years of service, he learned that while he was fighting the remaining Red Stick forces in Florida, his uncle had been killed at the Chechewa villages. The Lower Creek villagers were friendly to the United States, but Jackson failed to follow a direct order to destroy the town that came down from the Georgia governor, William Rabun. Rabun then ordered Captain Wright of the Georgia militia to destroy the village, and in doing so, Chief Howard was killed. This was another burden William carried on his already scarred back of allegiance to the United States. But it was also one that would start to change his mind about what side he would support.

The National Council was moved from Tuckabatchee to Broken Arrow, mainly because of the Indian Wars. McIntosh's popularity within the Creek nation was fading, but he still held a high place in power among the Creek chieftains in his hometown. As General Jackson and his army returned from the Florida campaign, where he was fighting the Seminoles, President James Monroe appointed a new Indian agent over the Creek territory, David B. Mitchell. Agent Mitchell met with fifteen of the Creek chiefs to negotiate yet another land purchase. Again, the discussion was not met with any optimism by the Indians. The Indians acknowledged that many of their laws had been broken, as were the promises of the United States, and proposed to rewrite the Creek laws in order to help encourage peace and finally end the Creek civil war.

The new laws of the Creeks did little to calm the fears of settlers, and Georgia was pushing for the total removal of all Indians. During this time, William McIntosh continued to encourage his followers to educate themselves in the white man's ways, to learn Christianity and to adopt European cultures. He knew, evidently, that all his people would be killed or removed from their homes one way or another.

On March 17, 1820, President Monroe asked the Senate to request money owed to the United States through debts acquired at the Wilkerson trading post. In this request, he indicated that the Indians had not paid their debts to Georgia and must therefore surrender the remaining territory in order to settle in arrears. This was a total fabrication and lie to gain the remaining territory and remove all the remaining Creek tribes once and for all. A meeting was arranged, and United States commissioners William McIntosh, Little Prince and several other chiefs met at the McIntosh Inn at Indian Springs to discuss the charges. The chiefs were outraged at the claims against them, and McIntosh stood firm in his resistance to accept that his people were guilty of any such action. He was, however, forced to recognize the debt of $500,000. In order to pay back the alleged debt that was conjured in the minds of political and land-hungry white men in Washington, the chiefs were, once again, forced to cede land to the government in order to settle the claim.

The treaty proposed the remaining territories were worth more than the alleged debt, and the Creeks were to receive $50,000 and a yearly payment of $150,000 for fourteen years. The Creeks also agreed to set aside one thousand acres for McIntosh, which caused speculation among the other chiefs that he was working only in favor of his own well-being and not on behalf of his people. David Mitchell was released from his duty as acting Indian agent, and he was replaced by John Crowell. Crowell forbade McIntosh from distributing any more annuities to the Creeks since he was funneling the money back into his own pocket by paying the Indians in large bills and forcing them to buy more goods than they actually needed from the McIntosh trading post. Thomas Crowell, John's brother, opened up a trading post as well and competed with McIntosh by cutting his prices. The competition eventually led Crowell to write to Big Warrior and Little Prince asking that McIntosh be dismissed as chief.

Crowell insisted that the remaining Creek Confederacy hold out against the threats of removal and not negotiate any new treaties. John Crowell fueled the fire that was slowly consuming William McIntosh. Meanwhile, Menawa was one of the remaining chiefs still hiding among the scattered Red Sticks. In 1823, McIntosh would bring all his demons to light by making one very fatal mistake: he underestimated the faith of his people and their unrelenting determination to hold on to their remaining lands. McIntosh was called on again to cede the land that Georgia had been promised for more than twenty years. A party was assembled to go west to the land in the proposed treaty and report back to the National Council, but the Cherokees there had no interest in selling. So McIntosh took it upon himself to write the chief a letter:

> *My friend; I am going to inform you in a few lines as a friend. I want you to give me your opinion about the treaty; whether the chiefs will be willing or not. If the chiefs feel disposed to let the United States have land, or part of it. I want you to let me know; I will make the United States Commissioners give you two thousand dollars, A. McCoy the same, and Charles Hicks three thousand dollars, for present, and nobody shall know it; and if you think the land would not be sold, I will get you the amount before the treaty sign; and if you get any friend you want him to receive, they shall receive. Nothing more to inform you at the present.*
>
>

I remain your affectionate friend,
William McIntosh

This fatal flaw in McIntosh's decision making solidified his true interest in the land treaties, and the letter was exposed in McIntosh's presence during the National Council when his military comrade read it out loud to the chiefs. This was no doubt a breaking point for the lowly chief. He dismissed himself from the council while his fellow tribesmen cursed him and dishonored his name.

Big Warrior and Little Prince lost all faith in McIntosh and proclaimed that no more land would be sold. They intended to stand against the United States and proclaim their right to stay. They also reenacted a previous Indian law that said that any chief who sold Creek land to the government would be killed. This proved to be a most effective tactic, and many of the chiefs now stood behind the original plan of their Upper Creek neighbors to oppose the land treaties. They also attacked McIntosh's integrity, and during the following year's National Council, which was also held at Broken Arrow, more than two hundred chiefs of the Creek and Cherokee Nations gathered to hear Big Warrior. Six thousand warriors were in attendance, and rumors of death were whispered to those who would sign the treaties. McIntosh was broken from the tribe and dismissed as speaker. When the state commissioners met to negotiate the land Georgia was still owed, the Indian council stood firm on its word not to negotiate. The commissioners warned the council that the native populations would be forcibly removed, but the chiefs still refused to sell.

After repeated attempts by the commissioners to persuade the Indians had failed, they reached out to William McIntosh. McIntosh had known for some time that the time would come when all the Indians would be removed. He favored the comforts of colonial living over the hardships of a migratory life but knew, deep down, the time was close. He used what little influence he had left to persuade a few chiefs in the Lower Creek towns to sign the Treaty of Indian Springs, releasing all the remaining territory in the Lower Creek towns to the U.S. government.

In mid-February 1825, a small council of about one hundred chiefs met with the United States commissioners to discuss and negotiate the Treaty of Indian Springs. Though many had come to witness the proverbial death warrant that was to be signed, after a few days, the agreement was made, and the chiefs supporting the land treaty lined up to literally sign away their lives. The threats to kill any chief who sold land were now inevitable. As Chief William McIntosh picked up the pen to sign the treaty, Opothle Yoholo, a Creek tribesman from the Cusseta town, stood on a rock outside the window and screamed at McIntosh. He angrily cursed him for his betrayal and yelled that McIntosh would die in his own blood. Nevertheless, the contract was signed, and the deed was done.

From that point on, William McIntosh was living on borrowed time. He knew that his life was at stake for what he had done. Chilly McIntosh, his son, heard a rumor that his father's demise was close and informed a runner to carry an urgent message to his father's plantation. On May 30, 1825, a small band of Creek warriors, led by the infamous Menawa, crept into the nearby woods at Acorn Bluff. Though the runner made it to McIntosh before the war party arrived, curiously, he did not leave. Menawa had sent word for his warriors to kidnap and hold Agent Hawkins as well. Hawkins was to be killed, but not until after they had disposed of McIntosh. The warriors were under orders to kill Chief William McIntosh according to the Creek customs: he had to be killed on his property and in front of his family.

In the early morning hours the following day, warriors descended on McIntosh's plantation and set it on fire. The choking flames and smoke woke the family, and William's wives and children were herded out the door, where they were grabbed up by the angry mob and dragged into the yard. The party stripped the children naked and threatened McIntosh with their lives if he did not show himself. Menawa shouted, "McIntosh, we have come! We have come! We told you if you sold the land to the government, we would come!" William's friend and old chief from Coweta Etomme Tustennuggee grabbed the rifles they had loaded previously in anticipation of the attack and fired at the group of Indians. Gunfire poured into the smoke-filled house, and the exchange of hot lead met William's friend, killing him. McIntosh was shot several times and fell to the floor. Menawa's men dragged him by his feet from the house, and William met his attackers with a face of stern defiance. In that moment, Menawa fiercely plunged his dagger into William's torso, gutting him like a pig. He was left to bleed out before he finally died. The raiders then scalped McIntosh, killed the livestock and burned the plantation to mere ashes.

McIntosh's legacy—for which he had fought, killed and lied—was now lying in ruins. His wives covered their bare children and sought shelter at a neighbor's house. The chief had given his final payment for his deeds and paid the ultimate price for turning his back on his people. That summer, the Creek Nation pardoned the remaining signers of the fraudulent treaty. McIntosh's death was an example for both the United States and the Creek Confederacy of how terrible the fight for Indian land had become. Andrew Jackson enforced the removal of the remaining natives from the territories and would later be recognized as a war hero and outstanding military leader. Jackson's recognition for his efforts in the Creek Wars paid minimal respect, if any, to the Muscogees, Cherokees, Choctaws and Seminoles who fought on behalf of the United States.

Starting in 1836, remnants of the poor and destitute Indians—left homeless, sick and tired from decades of hostilities, relocation and war—were forced from the southern Indian territories and gathered at Fort Mitchell in

Fort Mitchell was the location for Creek encampments while they awaited removal in 1836. This was one of the starting points for the Muscogee branch of the Trail of Tears.

Alabama. Thousands of native people, with little clothing, food, water or protection from the elements, were herded like cattle as they were forced to walk through seven hundred miles of uncharted wilderness. This would be the great American holocaust known as the Trail of Tears. They had nothing to look forward to and nowhere else to go. Hundreds died along the trail from starvation, disease, injury and exposure. Menawa, the old warrior who had fought so diligently to save his people, would also meet his fate on the trail. The crippled Creek Confederacy had done what it could to coexist with the settlers. But in the end, neither right nor wrong would prevail—only the greed and destruction of a government hell-bent on having its way.

The Land Thief and Indian Accomplice

Twenty years of bad land deals and encroachment in the Indian territories had become a serious and prominent issue by 1836. The removal of native people was coming to a close throughout the southern frontier, and the government clung to corrupt laws that swindled the remaining Muscogee people out of every last acre they had. As a result, all Indians in the territory who hadn't given up or sold their land freely were now being targeted by crooks and thieves. But it didn't stop there. The Creeks themselves also swindled their kinsman out of what they could in order to make a profit.

Because land fraud was ungoverned during America's infancy, the frontier was the perfect place for it to breed. With settlers taking over Georgia and Alabama regions, natives were left with little to fight over and even less to use as leverage to legally claim what was rightfully theirs. Because most of the tribes of the Coweta and Cusseta towns had already sold their lands, it wasn't difficult for small districts to be taken over by crooks seeking to gain land for profit and not necessarily for ownership.

Individual property deeds were issued by the United States land agents throughout the tribes in order to keep a record of what properties belonged to specific chiefs and tribes. To the Indians, the paper documents weren't necessarily valuable in any way. They were often sold or traded for next to nothing. The deeds were kept inside their clothing and often ruined after getting wet or stained and degraded with excessive wear to the point that they were illegible. This led to the loss of many of the documents, but agents still had to legally enforce the ownership of land and, in most cases, take the word of an Indian based on his knowledge of the property.

In the event that a debate arose over landownership, each party would have to produce witnesses to attest to ownership and swear, under oath, during testimony. With the closing days of removal, few, if any, native witnesses could be gathered to testify regarding the ownership of any property. Taking care of the deeds and the importance of their value was never properly communicated to the natives, and with the growing greed of the U.S. government for Indian land, a scandal evolved that would affect both frontier people and the few remaining Creek inhabitants.

Within the Cusseta towns of the Upper Creek region, many town chiefs had lost or disposed of the property deeds given to them by the land agents. The plan for removal had rooted many of the remaining people firmly in the ground. They would not leave unless they were forced or died defending their land. But this wouldn't be a problem for the crooked land thief and his Indian accomplice—especially since there was lots of money involved in a successful scam.

The land fraud scams were simple but effective. Disguised as a sophisticated resident of the Ucheetown, an Indian dressed in fine Victorian clothing, a silk hat and fine buckskin gloves would arrange to meet with the region's land agent to declare his ownership of land within

Land fraud was a serious scam during the 1800s. Indians who worked with settlers as accomplices disguised themselves as different members of neighboring towns in order to fool land agents out of property deeds. Those stolen deeds were later sold back to the United States government for three times the amount purchased. Pictured here are Jim Sawgrass and Swamp Owl of central Florida, descendants of the Seminole tribes.

a particular township and range. The agent would check his ledger for corresponding information, and if no one came forth to debate ownership of the property, within a few days, the agent would present the nicely dressed Indian with a deed to the property. In the same transaction, in the presence of the agent, the Indian would then sell the property to a buyer. In this manner, a man named John Williams, who was a known crook in the region, and his unknown Indian accomplice were able to scam several valuable certificates for Indian land.

Prior to this particular transaction, arrangements had been made between the Indian and John Williams for a portion of payment, which the Indian would receive for his part in the charade. Some time would lapse before the crooked couple would emerge again, but this time, the Indian accomplice would be in a different disguise to fool the government agent. With his rifle by his side, dressed in traditional chieftain's clothing, including a crown of beautiful turkey feathers, the Indian would present himself as O-ce-o-ho-la and tell the agent he was swimming across the Chattahoochee when he lost his deed in the water. Again, he would give the location of the property to the agent, who would check his roll. The information corresponded once more, and the buyer would show up to eagerly purchase the land from the crooked chief.

The two met for a third time with the agent—this time, to ratify an agreement between a poor Indian called Cho-fe, who, according to his story, had been away in a hunting party. During his venture, his deed was burned, and he needed a replacement in order to sell his property to Mr. John Williams. The Indian told the agent the town, district and plot of his land; there was no one to dispute the matter; and he subsequently sold his property to Mr. Williams. Again, the two crooks left the agent's office.

This type of criminal activity was costly for many Indians in the territory and something for which they would most definitely have killed their fellow tribesman. However, the idea of government control over land dictated ownership by law according to white men. When the legitimate owners of the land did finally present themselves before the land agent, the ratification of the contracts between the swindling John Williams and his mysterious Indian friend were already binding and legal, and the rightful owners were left with nothing. By the time representatives from Washington arrived to collect their land from the remaining Indians, Mr. Williams and his crooked Indian friend had invested a total of fifty dollars in their scam. However, they had swindled so many of the Creek people out of their lands that John had become a very rich man by selling them all to the government for an undisclosed amount of money.

Some of the remaining Creeks lived on plantations for a few years after the removal process began. They married into African American families, living and working as slaves for the very men who had taken their precious land from them. It was a heavy and burdened price to pay to stay in their homeland. Eventually, Indian agents would find their way to the plantations and rural pioneer settlements where the few remaining Indians were hiding. They, too, were promptly uprooted, taken from their new families and sent away with their kinsmen.

Baptized by Fire Water

The Native American populations throughout North America have been making intoxicating beverages and medicinal concoctions for thousands of years. The purpose of these spirits and medicines was mostly religious and ceremonial, but many types of herbal tonics, salves, powders, teas and foods were made as remedies for common ailments. Plants, leaves, roots and flowers were the medicine of ancient American people, and many of today's herbalists still use some of the traditional Indian medicines as an alternative source of natural healing.

Some of the southwestern Native Americans were known for their use of peyote, a species of cactus that grows in abundance near large deposits of limestone. This flowering cactus was often boiled into a tea or peeled and eaten. Indians believed the visions they had while under the influence of peyote came from their gods or spirit world. Many chiefs believed that communication with the spirit world could be obtained through these forms of trances to help guide them, make important decisions for their tribes or prosper in battle. Wild mushrooms (of the psilocybin species) are more commonly known today as "magic mushrooms," a term coined in the 1960s among hippie cultures. The hallucinogenic quality of the fungus causes a state of lucid dreaming and heightens the senses, especially audible sounds, leading many users to believe that they can converse with supernatural forces. The image of this medicinal fungus has also been depicted in cave art throughout the southern regions of the United States.

Wild flowers and plants that grow in many parts of the southern United States were also used to induce euphoric states of enlightenment and for ceremonial purposes. Morning glory, cannabis and salvia are all plants that were used in cleansing and smoke ceremonies. The leaves, seeds and flowers were used for different tonics, smoked or consumed raw in order to reach the divine. One such flower of the nightshade variety, known as jimson weed, got its name from a strange case of accidental poisoning in the Virginia Colony of Jamestown.

In 1607, the colony of Jamestown, Virginia, was settled by the Virginia Company of London as a district of England. Many impoverished English families made their way to the New World as indentured servants, and the colony was highly profitable in tobacco. Over the years, higher taxes and the decline in tobacco sales caused the poor frontier farmer to push farther into Indian territories, resulting in feuds between settlers and native people. By 1675, hostilities and uprising in Virginia had caused a farmer named Nathanial Bacon to organize a small band of men to fight against the Susquehannok, a tribe of the Iroquois.

Bacon was denied a military commission by the royal governor, Sir William Berkley, to continue his war against the natives. Berkley believed that an Indian war would disrupt the fur trading between settlers and

Nathaniel Bacon, of the Virginia Colony, led a rebellion against the
Iroquois in 1676. During his campaign, soldiers were accidently poisoned
by consuming jimson weed.

natives, as well as hurt his political standing among the Jamestown elite. Bacon
led his rebellion anyway and continued to fight the Indians. In 1676, when
Bacon's renegade militia returned from a campaign, a meal was prepared
for the soldiers. A salad, infused with the nightshade flower, was part of that
meal, and the men promptly consumed it. Shortly after, they began to show
signs of severe hallucinations. One man sat in a corner naked, folded his
arms like a bird and made animal sounds at the other men. Another would
caress and kiss everyone he met, and others were prevented from rolling in
their own feces, which to them seemed a pleasant thing do to at the time.

The circumstances of this particular episode of accidental poisoning were documented as "a very pleasant comedy for they turned natural fools upon it for several days. A thousand such simple tricks they played, and after 11 days returned themselves again, not remembering anything had passed."

These types of natural entheogens (a word classifying a group of plants that generate or stimulate hallucinations, euphoric effects or trance-like states) are still used today for some ceremonial purposes in aboriginal tribes but are mostly illegal in the United States. However, with the outlawing of herbal plants, even for medicinal purposes, came the popular trend of distilling spirits.

Absinthe, widely known as the "Green Fairy" for its signature green color, is derived from wormwood. Wormwood is an ornamental plant indigenous to North Africa and Eurasia. When consumed as a spirit, thujone, a psychochemical present in the drink, can cause effects of clear-headed euphoria or lucid drunkenness. Famous painters like Vincent Van Gough were avid absinthe drinkers, along with Oscar Wilde, the famed Irish poet and writer who was often vilified when he consumed too much of the musing spirit.

Among the Indian territories, in the frontier days of Alabama, growing populations of European immigrants mixed with the native populations. New foods, clothing, goods and implements were becoming customary and even necessary for trading and bargaining between settlers and Indians. Exotic jewelry and furs from unusual animals became a luxury in frontier settlements, while foreign food and drink became popular with the indigenous people. One particular drink of which Indians became very fond was distilled liquor and whiskey or, as they called it, "fire water."

Throughout the United States, distilled alcohol has been a historical staple for generations of frontier people. The Appalachian regions and southern states are most commonly thought of when people bring up the subject of moonshine. The name itself can be associated with outlaw drivers and backwoods mountain men (and women) who made substantial livings from distilling and transporting alcohol from place to place. Some of the earliest accounts of frontier people trading alcohol to the Indians in Russell County are far from pleasant. Even by historical accounts, the problem with alcoholism became a rampant issue during the early days of the frontier South.

Absinthe is a spirit that was popular with artists like Vincent Van Gough and the famous Irish poet Oscar Wilde. The effects of this spirit are described as lucid dreaming or clear-headed drunkenness. *Courtesy of the Library of Congress.*

The Murder of Joe Marshall: 1833

Within the Creek territories lived many mixed-blood Indians who were often some of the wealthiest men in the region. Joe Marshall and his brothers, Benjamin and Jim, were mixed Creek chieftains of the Lower Creek towns who lived in what is today Russell County. Benjamin lived in Brownville (which would have been located in Phenix City today) and established a ferry near Fort Mitchell that served as one of the only means of safely crossing the Chattahoochee River. Joe Marshall lived just east of Salem in what is today Lee County on a plantation where he owned many slaves. He was considered among his social class to be hospitable and courteous to everyone, including the white settlers. According to old documents found in historical books about the Marshalls, Joe and his brothers often took their white neighbors with them as guests to the Indian ballgames, which were held near the location of Wacoochee. They joined them for the Green-Corn dances at the ceremonial grounds and went to meetings at the Creek council house once located near Moffett's Mill in Salem.

Close to the location that was Moffett's Mill in Salem, Alabama, there once stood an Indian council house where many Creek chiefs of the Lower Towns met and conducted business. Ben Marshall was one of those mixed-race chiefs who frequently took his neighbors to Green-Corn ceremonies and Indian town meetings. *Courtesy of the Library of Congress.*

Because Joe Marshall was among the Creek mixed bloods, he often found himself torn between his ancestral customs and the ways of white men. However, it was (and still is) customary for members of the tribe to take in the children of their kin or tribe in the event of death or if something were to happen to them. Joe took in a young boy named Eas-ko, but he was referred to in historical records by his Christian name, Josiah. Joe raised him as his own, and like his own children, he became part of the Marshall family. Sometime during 1833, when Josiah was a young man, he had an argument with another Indian over whiskey. Just a short time after the argument occurred, Josiah went on a drunken rampage and vowed to kill the man over the matter. When he had drunk himself to inebriation, he sat down near a tree on the road on which he knew his foe would be traveling. The location was near "Henry Gibson's field," in what is today Smiths Station. He waited for a short time and then spotted the liquor-thieving bandit as he approached. Josiah raised his rifle and set his iron sights on his victim. Without the clarity or consciousness of a sober man, he shot him down in cold blood, killing him instantly. Unfortunately, the man Josiah shot was not the man with whom he had argued; rather, it was his friend and adopted father, Joe Marshall.

Josiah was arrested for the murder of Joe Marshall and brought to the village of Girard by Sheriff George W. Elliot. According to historical accounts, Josiah was noticeably upset that he had accidently killed his friend instead of his intended target. When Sheriff Elliot placed his prisoner behind bars, Josiah said, "Are you going to kill Indian now?" Elliot responded, "Oh no." Then the inmate asked, "Well; you no kill Indian now, give Indian something to eat."

Josiah was executed in a public hanging in Girard for his crime, and his execution is one of the first recorded hangings documented in Russell County. It's rumored that the stump of the tree where the murder took place can still be seen on the property. It serves as a haunting reminder of the men who died under the noose of justice and that nothing good ever came out of the bottom of a whiskey jug.

Uncle Blake's Recollection of Indian Justice: 1834

In 1834, land near the little Uchee River that belonged to the Lower Creeks was quickly being consumed by the Columbus Land Company. The council house, located near Moffett's Mill, was still being used by the Indians, who were struggling to come to terms with the encroachment of settlers and the impending removal of all Indians.

A.B. Thomas, who was also known to many in the region as "Uncle Blake," traveled the Derrysall Trail from Harris County, Georgia, to the frontier settlements in Alabama with his new bride. They built their home about eight miles south of Salem, Alabama. At the time, this area was part of Russell County, and the frontier settlements there were growing rapidly. Though he was a white man, Thomas was familiar with the Creeks and their language. He had lived among them without disruptions or hardship for most of his life in Georgia. During his migration, he came to the northern point of the Salem settlement that crossed the Little Uchee Creek. With his wagon full of his family's belongings, he struggled to get his oxen to cross the water. When they reached the midpoint of the creek, the oxen stalled, and he was forced to leave his frail wife and wagon standing in the water to go find help.

Uncle Blake spotted a home located about three hundred yards from the creek and went to ask the owner for a shovel in order to dig out his wagon. Once he acquired the necessary tools, he noticed several Indians approaching the house. This was a bit unusual, but since Blake spoke their language, he asked them to help him, and they eagerly agreed. As they approached the wagon, one of the Indians spotted the brim of a whiskey jug wrapped in canvas and asked for a drink. The whiskey was used as a medicinal tonic for Mrs. Blake, who suffered from chronic poor health. However, knowing the natives' love for fire water, he knew that denying them their requests could result in fatal consequences. Uncle Blake allowed them all to partake, and they quickly pushed the wagon across the river and up the bank.

One of the young Indian men was sporting a handsome, silver-plated rifle. The rifle was one of extraordinary craftsmanship and wasn't a typical possession among the mostly poor Indian population of the time. One of the Indians turned to Blake and said, "We-waugh-we-hart-a-h-la-wap," which roughly translated to "We have been in the water and done an unpleasant job." This meant that the Indian wanted another drink. Only this time, Uncle Blake denied them. Still, they insisted, and the Indian sporting the fine silver rifle pulled a tin cup from his waistband and placed one silver dollar inside it. He offered the cup to Blake so that he would remove the dollar and fill the cup with whiskey. The cup held only about four ounces. A dollar for four ounces was more than a bargain, and Blake readily filled his cup and took the money. In doing so, the Indian treated his four companions to the same.

As the Thomas family sat in their cabin, they could see through the crumbling clay mortar in the walls. Several natives were surrounding the house. Suddenly, a young Indian man burst through the front door and attempted to hide as a group of angry assailants followed him. They apprehended him and administered a form of justice that should have killed the young man.

A short time later, Mrs. Blake was cooking supper when she began to notice Indians running around her home. As she peered through the cracks of the log cabin, she could see about twenty or more Indians gathering in her yard. Suddenly, the young Indian man who had been so generous with his money came bursting through the door. He had a look of panic on his face, and he tried to hide under a table as several of the other Indians rushed in to apprehend him. They dragged the young man out, kicking, screaming and flailing about. The angry mob of intuders then searched the young man and found about $400 in silver specie (a name used for coinage). They took it along with the fancy rifle he was carrying.

According to the account by Blake, the young Indian man had stolen the money and the rifle from a chief just a week before. The chief was visiting the council house of Tus-koo-na Fix-a-ko and was very upset that his money and fine possessions had been stolen. Creek tribesmen were made aware of the situation and were appointed to administer justice if and when they discovered the culprit.

As Blake followed the group of Indians and their hostage into the woods, he observed a manner of justice he could explain only as "the most terrible beating inflicted upon a living creature—man or beast—that did not die from the effects of it." The Indians tied the young man to a fallen hickory tree, and each one of them administered blow after blow to the body, head and extremities of the man. Large, sturdy branches were used to beat the poor Indian man until his face was nearly unrecognizable. The merciless beating went on for several hours, and the man was finally cut loose and left for dead. Uncle Blake did note that the Indian thief survived the ordeal but was never seen or heard from again. Blake may have made the right choice not to ruffle the feathers of the Indians near his settlement, for Indian justice can come swifter than eagles.

The Murder of "Indian" Joe Conard: 1835

It was April Fool's Day 1835 when Cyrus Cotton, a wealthy grocer and liquor distributor in Russell County, opened the doors of his general store for business as usual. He had made a small fortune in the mercantile business and was not opposed to selling liquor to anyone if it made him a bit of money. Cotton was especially fond of his Indian customers, who were among the regulars who came to purchase the liquor they so dearly loved.

That morning, an Indian named A-Cee, also known by his Christian name, Joe Conard, came into Cotton's store to purchase a jug of whiskey. The two had a disagreement over a debt, and Joe Conard left without his purchase. Presumably, this was nothing for Cyrus Cotton to be upset over, as he had many customers and a flourishing business, so he conducted his work and went home that evening. As nightfall approached, just before dinner, Cotton was standing in his room, combing his hair in the mirror. A gunshot rang out across the house as a bullet split the windowpanes and met Cotton in the neck, tearing away the flesh about an inch deep. Cotton and his friend, who was staying with him, quickly examined the wound and dressed it appropriately. Not understanding why or how he had been attacked, Cotton and a servant saddled their horses and rode more than twenty miles to the nearby city of Columbus, Georgia. There, the men stayed with Cotton's family for two weeks, trying to figure out who had attempted to kill him.

Cotton finally returned to his home, which was located on the banks of the Little Uchee. He reopened his business and treated the Indians to whatever they wanted. This was his way of fishing out his attacker. He knew that one of his native customers would eventually tell him who had attempted to assassinate him. The obvious suspect was Joe Conard, the Indian with whom Cotton had quarreled. Cotton was convinced Conrad was to blame and was disgusted over the ordeal, especially since he had been so generous with the Indians. But Joe Conard was nowhere to be found.

The local magistrate appointed Cyrus Cotton to the role of sheriff, and Conard was eventually located and arrested. When he was apprehended, the deputies tied him up with rope and took him to Girard to be formally charged with attempted murder. Cotton notified his friends of Conard's arrest, and they joined him as escorts to Girard. Only Conard never made it to Girard, and neither did Cotton or his deputized posse.

Hearing gunfire on the trail, some Indians in the area, curiously and cautiously, migrated in the direction of the racket. When they arrived, they found the body of A-Cee—Joe Conard—dead and tied to a tree, his body filled with several bullets. There was no one around, but they believed that Cotton and his posse were to blame. The Indians caught up with Cotton and his men on the trail and secretly followed them as they bypassed Girard and rode into Columbus.

More than six months passed before Cotton was arrested in October 1835. He was charged with the murder of Joe Conard, and the Creek chiefs insisted that he be tried in their tribal courts, which would have resulted in death for Cotton. He was arrested by the local sheriff and tried for murder in Girard. As a result, his initial $10,000 bond was dropped to only $500, and he remained in jail as a precautionary measure rather than as an inmate for his crime. The hostilities between whites and Indians had risen to a detrimental level in 1835 and 1836. Raids and murders were so prevalent in the county that court time and trials were kept short, and very little information was actually being documented through the judicial system.

By the time 1837 arrived, the *Conard v. Cotton* case had been bounced from court to court until the fines had dwindled to nearly nothing. Cotton's case was dismissed when the solicitor declined to prosecute the case further. Leaving no vindication for Joe Conard, Cyrus Cotton had gotten away with murder.

Tragedy and Traitors

The Edwards families moved from Talbot, Georgia, to Russell County, Alabama, in 1834. Brothers Loxla and Berry Edwards settled in a small region that is today Lee County. Loxla ran a small general store and traded with the Indians who also lived in the area. After a few months, he moved to another location near Springvilla, where two of his sons, John and James, already lived. There, he built a plantation and mill along the Edwards Creek. His younger brother, Berry, was a farmer, and he also settled near Edwards Creek after his home in Georgia was destroyed in an Indian raid.

During 1834, the Edwards families lived without concern for their Indian neighbors. They welcomed them to their homes and treated them with much respect and kindness. In fact, several of the local chiefs considered the Edwardses good friends; their children played together, and the local Indians helped watch over their homes and livestock. This all changed in 1836, when the Indian removal times were at hand. With many of the poor and destitute Indian families living in harsh conditions, they often resorted to criminal acts out of spite and, sometimes, necessity.

At the pioneer home of Loxla Edwards, it wasn't uncommon for local Indians to approach the house without apprehension or need to worry. The Edwards children had grown accustomed to greeting them, and most of the time, they had no reason to fear them at all. Caroline Edwards, Loxla's ten-year-old daughter, was playing in the front yard when she noticed a drunken Indian staggering across the lawn. Being young and very naïve to the Indians' state of mind, she approached him and began to chase him about the yard. Mr. Edwards noticed the man and thought he might be a visitor. As he walked toward him to greet him, he was horrified when the man suddenly grabbed Caroline by the hair and flung her over a small stump, raising his axe to decapitate her.

Caroline screamed as her vicious attacker lowered his tomahawk. Loxla grabbed the drunken man from behind and violently threw him to the ground. As the drunken Indian struggled to get up, Loxla piled several heavy logs on him to prevent him from escaping. Loxla's anger had convinced him to set fire to the logs and burn the man alive for the attempted murder of his daughter, but in the aftermath, he knew that the current condition of the frontier would likely lead to retaliation from the local natives. So against his own judgment, he convinced the Indian he would not kill him if he stayed away from his home and he never saw him again.

Berry Edwards's encounters with the Indians in the frontier territories were also unsettling and often tragic. His children, like his brother's, were also very used to being around their Creek neighbors on the frontier. This changed for Berry Edwards's family as well when his seven-year-old son, Jimmie, was shot and killed by an Indian they knew named Pen Cally. The children were leaving the turnip patch when they saw Pen sitting in the garden, eating the turnips. They suspected no harm or bad intentions from the man since they knew him. As the children were crossing the creek on their way home, Pen emerged with a rifle and shot the little boy just below the shoulder. Little Jimmie later died from the wound. Upon his son's death, Berry Edwards immediately formed a posse to apprehend the murderer. They quickly caught up to Pen and took him into custody. They were headed to Columbus, Georgia, to turn him into the stockade when Pen escaped and was never heard from again.

It was the summer of 1836 when Berry Edwards himself would encounter the Indians for the last time. He had planted a crop that May and, shortly after, organized to relocate his family to Georgia in an effort to keep them safe from the Indian outbreaks that were occurring all over the frontier. He returned in late summer and was harvesting his crop when he and his friend were ambushed by a band of Indians. A neighbor heard the gunfire and reported the incident to authorities in Columbus that night. Soldiers were dispatched to follow up on the situation and found Berry Edwards's lifeless body slumped over the wash bench in a nearby spring. He was apparently shot and ran as far as the spring before he collapsed and died. His friend Alexander Goolsby was found about a quarter of a mile into the woods, where he, too, had been shot and killed.

During the close of the Civil War, around 1865, as General James Wilson and his notorious raiders ripped through the Lee and Russell County regions of Alabama on their way to Columbus, a group of six Union deserters joined a local resident who lived in the county and began to raid, plunder and terrorize the families who lived there. On a Sunday morning, just as Loxla Edwards and his family were loading into their wagon to head to church, the band of miscreants held the family at gun and knife point and tormented and tortured them for hours.

The group demanded that Loxla Edwards hand over any valuables or money he had. He bluntly told the men that he had nothing of value and no money to give. Again, they demanded valuables, holding a sword to Mrs. Edwards's neck and advising her not to scream or she'd have her throat slit from one end to the other. Mr. Edwards pleaded with them as they

General James Wilson rode through Russell County, Alabama, in the spring of 1865. Six of his men deserted the company and formed an outlaw band with a local man. The outlaws tormented and brutally assaulted families who lived in the rural communities. *Courtesy of the Library of Congress.*

continued to prod him for the whereabouts of his valuables. One man took a rope from his horse and fashioned a noose out of it. They placed it around Mr. Edwards's neck in an effort to loosen his tongue, but he still insisted he had nothing to give. This wasn't what the wicked men wanted to hear, so they threw the noose over the nearest tree and slowly began to string him up. They let him hang for several minutes, almost choking him to death. When they lowered him down, he continued to insist he had nothing. A second time, the men pulled him up on the noose. The rope began to shift and burn Mr. Edwards as he flailed and gasped for breath. His wife and children, debilitated by fear, had no choice but to watch as he was brutally tortured. When his assailants let him down again, they demanded money and jewelry. As before, Loxla told them he had none. So for the third time, the villains pulled hard, as they intended to kill Mr. Edwards once and for all. He dangled for several minutes until the pleas of his wife and children were heard by several of the Edwardses' servants.

Two field hands, Charles and Dave, along with the family's house maid, Miss Frances, ran out to the mob of men and pleaded with them to let Mr.

Edwards down. They all insisted that there was no money or anything of value that they could take. At that time, the band of evil men cut Loxla Edwards down from the noose. He was nearly unconscious but was able to be revived quickly. The bandits entered Mr. Edwards's home and took everything they could carry, including a sword that belonged to his brother. They plundered his kitchen for food, as well as clothing, taking with them boots and jackets. At sundown, they left the Edwards plantation to carry on their horrible escapade. It's uncertain whether those men who rode with the Yankee butcher were ever apprehened or charged for their crimes.

The last tragedy that cursed the Edwards family took place on a beautiful May afternoon in 1865. The Edwards families, along with their neighbors, were gathered for an afternoon picnic at the Edwards Mill. The reunion was to celebrate the return of the community's soldiers from the battlefields of the Civil War. Several creeks joined at the mill, and a small bateau (flat-bottomed riverboat) was the only means of crossing the deep water. Berry (Loxla's thirty-two-year-old son); his sister, Olivia; and his sixteen-year-old nieces, Maxie and Minerva Brooks, boarded the fragile boat with another family friend and set out across the water. The little boat capsized about halfway into the creek, dumping its passengers into the water. They drowned in the sharp current, and there was nothing that could be done to save them. Their families watched helplessly from the banks as the five of them drowned.

Loxla died in 1880. His remaining children lived in and around their family plantation for many years afterward. One of Loxla's sons, James Polk Edwards, would become a sheriff in Lee County and a probate judge and served as the mayor of Opelika in 1875, 1876 and 1877. His attitude toward maintaining the dignity of his community through enforcing the law may have come as a result of his personal experiences and tragedy at the hands of criminals and growing up on the Alabama frontier.

Chattahoochee River Raiders

On both sides of the Chattahoochee River, the shoals brought together neighboring Muscogee tribes for fishing and recreation. Women and girls brought hand-woven baskets and fish traps to catch the shad, bass and sunfish that were abundant here. Young boys, skilled in bow fishing, accurately speared large catfish in the shallows, and some even lassoed huge lake sturgeon and brought them to shore. Children played in the cool baths of the Chattahoochee, which were a welcoming relief in the spring and summer when daytime temperatures could be as high as eighty and ninety degrees.

The Uchee Creek tribes lived along the Chattahoochee River and were known for their hostile nature just prior to removal. Their village was known as a "war town" in the Creek territory, and though these tribes were relatively different from the Cow Creeks who shared the river region in the Lower Creek town of Coweta, they lived very much the same way. They all depended on farming, fishing and gathering to provide for their people.

In the sixteenth century, voyagers and explorers from England, Spain and France found their way to the Indian towns that were located on the Chattahoochee River. The Spanish fought with the Uchees for allegiance, and in the early seventeenth century, they burned the Indian cities, forcing the Creek people to relocate. The Coweta people moved to an area that is today located in Macon, Georgia, on the Ocmulgee River. Later, after the Yamasee War of 1715, the native people were forced to relocate once more and settled again on the Chattahoochee near the Coweta Falls in the early 1800s.

Years of relocating and constant uprisings against invaders and European settlers would make life very difficult for the Muscogee people, splitting the native nation into separate sects. The New or Upper Creek tribes were located upriver from the Coweta town. The Lower Creeks were descendants of the original Coweta people, who were already mixed into a few white settlements in the area, giving them an advantage over their Upper Creek neighbors, who did not want to integrate into white society. The Indian way of life was slowly dying, and new European settlements were forcing the Creek people out of their homeland and ancestral regions. Once the laws of white men were imposed on the native populations, the common Indian would become a common criminal.

Under the command of the infamous Creek chief Jim Henry, a band of renegade Creeks from the Coweta and war towns formed a war party on Friday, May 13, 1836. The group of perfidious and angry natives began their attack on two steamboats that were harbored in the Chattahoochee River. The *Georgian* was attacked first. The assailants quickly and quietly boarded the ship. Then the angry mob began to unleash an attack on the passengers. They wielded tomahawks and stone blades at their victims, until nearly every person on board was dead. The engineer was the lone survivor and narrowly escaped when the ship was set on fire. The *Hyperian* was anchored just two miles up the river from where the *Georgian* was attacked. In the same stealthy manner, the Indians boarded and launched a relentless

Steamships were a common means of transportation along the Chattahoochee River during the frontier days. During Indian attacks and raids, these ships were often targeted in an effort to prevent escape. *Courtesy of the Library of Congress.*

assault on the passengers, killing as many as they could. The ship was set afloat, and it drifted until it hit a sandbar. Only the captain and two women managed to escape.

The outlaw group crossed the Chattahoochee River on May 14 and descended on the unassuming settlement of Roanoke, Georgia, in Stewart County that night. Reports from the small militia force set up to defend the settlement said that strange hoots emanated from the nearby forests that evening. Many of the soldiers dismissed the unusual sounds as overactive spring fowl, perhaps mating or fighting. The soldiers had no idea they were being surrounded by the same murderous group of Indians who had attacked the steamers the day before.

The tiny community in Roanoke was known as "Little Hamlet," and most of the reports that stem from this particular event suggest that the camp was relatively quiet that night and the militia troops retired to their camp houses, and so did the inhabitants of the town. In the early morning hours of May 15, 1836, the settlers of this quiet community, who lay sleeping in their beds, had no idea what terror awaited them. As the war party of Indians approached the settlement, under the cover of a pre-morning fog, they entered the town of Roanoke, and a vicious and malevolent intrusion ensued as they rained down a hail of gunfire and assaults on every man, woman and child they could find.

Within a short length of time, the raiders had killed and scalped nearly every inhabitant of Little Hamlet, leaving very few survivors. The town was burned to ashes, and those who did survive were injured and terribly maimed. Many of the townspeople were also missing—a cruel and brutal reminder of how dangerous frontier life really was.

Shortly after this atrocity, most of the rogue tribe was apprehended and sent to different locations for imprisonment until trial. Six of the Indians involved in the raid at Roanoke were captured near Columbus, Georgia, and were tried and sentenced to hang for murder. On the morning of November 26, 1836, Co-in-chi-na, Tus-coo-ner, Clis-ar-ne-ha and Tim-a-sc-ha (four of the six Creek warriors) were hanged in an area located on the Alabama side of the Chattahoochee River, close to the Dillingham Street Bridge. Reports from those who witnessed this public execution said the warriors died very heroic deaths. They stood tall like the great bear and welcomed death as if it were a close friend—a common trait among Indian warriors. This location would later become one of Girard's most lawless villages.

II

SODOM

The Lawless Village of Girard

Establishing Girard

Girard, Alabama, was named for Philadelphia philanthropist Stephen Girard. He was born in Bordeaux, France, in 1750 and spent most of his life sailing the Caribbean with his father, who was a captain. When he was eight years old, he lost sight in his right eye and had very little education. Still, he managed to become one of America's wealthiest individuals. In 1812, he opened several branches of Girard Banks all over Philadelphia, Pennsylvania. His contributions to the United States helped keep the government stable, and he singlehandedly financed the War of 1812, supplying 95 percent of the financial backing needed to keep the war active. He was also noted for his monumental contributions to orphans, particularly those of coal miners. On December 22, 1830, at the age of eighty-one, Girard was crossing the street in Philadelphia and was run over by a horse and carriage. The accident damaged his other eye and tore open his face. He managed to survive the incident but never fully recovered from his injuries. A year later, on December 26, 1831, he died and was buried in the Holy Trinity Catholic Cemetery in Philadelphia.

Stephen Girard purchased much of the Creek territory that would become Russell County before his death. The name Girard was given to the small settlement in the old Indian territory near Coweta Village in 1832. It was originally the location of the reserve of Benjamin Marshall, a mixed-blood Indian chief who lived in the region among his people in the Lower Creek

The settlement of Girard, Alabama, was named for wealthy Philadelphia philanthropist Stephen Girard. Girard singlehandedly financed the Indian Wars in 1812. *Courtesy of the Library of Congress.*

towns. The reserve spanned the distance of the Chattahoochee River from what is today Fifteenth Street in Phenix City to Fort Mitchell, Alabama. Marshall sold his reserve for $35,000 to the Columbus Real Estate Company. Later, the company sold the property for $100,000, and the region known today as Russell County was established. In December 1832, the county seat was moved to Girard, and frontier settlers started to migrate farther into the area to establish plantations and larger communities.

Creek chieftains who lived in the region were among those wealthy enough to maintain their plantations. Paddy Carr was one of those chiefs, and he owned several hundred acres, as well as plantations and fine homes. He also owned many slaves and was part of the extended family of elite Creeks who lived in what are now Lee and Russell Counties. Benjamin Marshall's home was also located in an area that was known as Brownville. Brownville was established in 1883, after Girard, in the northern part of the county in what is today Lee County.

Among the first white settlers to live in this mostly Indian region of Alabama were John Godwin and his family. Godwin was a very successful architect and builder who made a name for himself in Girard and Columbus, Georgia, building most of the homes in the area. When he moved to Girard in October 1832, he brought with him the slave families from his former plantation. One of those slaves was a man named Horace King. King was born to a family of Creoles who had intermarried into the Catawba tribes near the Cheraw District in South Carolina. He was twenty-five years old when the Godwin family moved to Alabama, and he established himself as a valuable business partner to Godwin.

King was an extraordinary bridge builder. He completed the construction of his first bridge over the Pee Dee River in South Carolina before moving to Girard. While living and working in Alabama, he built all the original bridges that spanned the distance of the Chattahoochee River from Girard to Columbus. These include the lower wagon bridge (Dillingham Street Bridge), which was rebuilt by King after the flood of 1838; the factory bridges that connected the Columbus Navy Yard, the Ironworks and the Eagle Phenix Mills to Girard; and the railroad bridges that brought tremendous growth to Girard and Columbus by opening the cities to railroad transportation.

In February 1848, Godwin decided to emancipate Horace King in Tuscaloosa, Alabama. King's freedom never led him from his sense of obligation regarding his work. He rebuilt bridges and honored Godwin's previous contracts to build and repair bridges they had worked on together. The original wagon bridge was destroyed in 1865, during the Battle of Girard. The factory and railroad bridges were built in 1866, totaling $51,000, making Horace King a very wealthy man, as well as one of Girard's most valuable citizens. He was respected for his superior intellect and humble demeanor.

Girard was evolving from a frontier town into a thriving community. However, on the west side of the river, just short of a mile from the lower wagon bridge, there was a small settlement that was considered, at best, the filthiest place in the entire world. A few renegades, white men of lower classes, runaway slaves, drunkards and poor Indians built a shanty town of

Horace King was born into a family of Creole slaves near the Cheraw District in South Carolina. He was twenty-five years old when he moved with the Godwin family to Alabama. He later established himself as a valuable business partner to John Godwin and has been recognized for his superior building skills and political contributions.

shotgun shacks for gambling, prostitution, a grocery (that most often sold bad liquor) and hideouts for outlaws. This diabolical combination of cutthroats and criminals catered to the darkest pleasures of men, and the little village of Girard was shadowed by the devil himself as he beckoned sinners like the sirens of Homer's *Odyssey*.

In 1833, a Christian minister visiting the small village in Girard, not believing a place could be as deplorable and crime stricken as the community said, witnessed the violence and lawlessness of the little shanty village and stated, "This is Sodom," comparing it to the biblical city along the Jordan River in Canaan that was condemned by God for its sin and destroyed by fire and brimstone. The nickname "Sodom" stuck with the filth and scum that accumulated in Girard. Historian and Reverend Francis Lafayette Cherry wrote:

> *Girard was originally what might be compared to a cess-pool, which received the scum and filth from Columbus, it being in a different State violators of order and decorum found it a convenient and measurably secure*

place of refuge from the majesty of the law. Here, in consequence of the lawless condition of the country at the period, was collected a conglomerated mixture of gambler, black-leg, murderer, thief and drunkard, all of whom, mingled together indiscriminately, produced a moral odor so offensive to the very idea of good morals, and secured for the place, for several years, the appellation of "Sodom," which in all probability, it well deserved.

With the growing crime in the village of Girard, law enforcement was established to protect law-abiding citizens from the criminals who were making the refuge of Sodom their halfway home. Because the frontier days limited the resources of the citizens of Girard, court was often held on the front lawn of the Golding family estate, which neighbored the property of John Godwin. Godwin's workshops were also used as courtrooms and offices for attorneys. This primitive means of prosecution was all the citizens of Girard had to work with, so they made do with whatever they could to uphold the law.

Some of the earliest court cases on Russell County dockets are listed as such: Eliza Bland, October 13, 1833, arrested for playing cards and betting on them in a public place; James Simmons arrested for betting on dice; Peter C. Perkins and an associate were fined fifty and forty dollars, respectively, for terrorizing the public while carving each other up in a knife fight; William Gray and Enoch Johnson were both jailed and fined for selling whiskey, rum and gin without a license; an Indian woman known as "Mollie," who was a resident of Sodom (her Christian name was Gracy Slate), appeared on the prisoner docket almost every day in 1833 for keeping a disorderly house; and a neighbor, Sam Brown, was charged and sentenced to hang for stealing slaves in 1836.

Though some of the crimes listed seem petty by today's standards, there were far worse atrocities that took place in Girard that kept the local magistrate busy. One of the most recognized cases of defiance between military and civil justice was the murder case of Hardeman Owen.

Hardeman Owen was born in Oglethorpe, Georgia, on November 11, 1800. He lived in the Muscogee Territory and was known for his brutal and terrible behavior toward Indians. He frequently harassed, beat, maimed and killed the natives if they refused to surrender or move off their land. He was also surveying much of the Indian Territory for gold, which added to the greed that enticed settlers to move farther into Creek territory. Those settlers were openly violating the 1814 Treaty of Fort Jackson, which was designed to protect the Indians from having their land taken by force. Also, the garrison that manned Fort Mitchell from 1825 until 1840 was ordered to protect those vulnerable natives. Regardless of treaties and laws, the native people were at the mercy of the United States government, as well as the frontier settlers. Often, the retaliation of Indians against the settlers would lead to the arrest and immediate execution of Indians who were captured during raids or fighting that broke out between groups.

Owen's notorious behavior and bad treatment of the Creek Indians earned him a warrant for arrest, and a federal marshal was dispatched from Washington to serve and apprehend him. When he heard that federal agents were looking for him, he planned to meet the marshal at his home. However, Hardeman Owen would not give up his freedom so easily. On the day Owen arranged to meet the marshal, he placed a black powder keg with a smoldering fuse under his house. The idea was that the U.S. marshal would arrive and find Owen's home empty, at which point he would be killed in an explosion. A local Indian, who was friendly to the agents, warned the U.S. marshal, and the marshal did not enter Hardeman's home. The house did in fact blow up, scattering the Owen homestead for miles.

Now the marshal had another reason to find Hardeman Owen, and another warrant was issued for the attempted murder of a government agent. Since the nature of the situation had escalated to such a dangerous level, the marshal went to Fort Mitchell, where he requested a unit of armed militia to help him apprehend his man. His request was granted, and on July 30, 1833, the marshal and militia caught up to Owen. During the arrest, the soldiers drew arms against Owen and demanded he surrender to the marshal for his crimes. He refused, and a gunfight ensued. One of the soldiers fired at Owen, killing him.

Though the Indian citizens of the territory were relieved to know Hardeman Owen had been killed, white citizens were outraged and demanded that the soldier who killed Owen be arrested. General Jas. J. McIntosh harbored the soldiers who killed the Indian butcher at Fort Mitchell. When the sheriff arrived to arrest the men, he demanded that McIntosh turn them over, to which McIntosh replied, "I'll be damned if I give up a man." Shortly afterward, a warrant was also issued against General McIntosh for contempt.

James Emmerson, James King, David Manning and Jeremiah Austil were all arrested and charged with the murder of Hardeman Owen. Because the men were soldiers, a request for military representation was sent to Washington. The attorney who represented the men during their trial in the winter of 1833 was none other than Francis Scott Key. He was sent to

After Hardeman Owen was killed, the soldiers who were involved were sent back to Fort Mitchell. When local authorities came to apprehend the men, General McIntosh refused to turn them over. He told the sheriff, "I'll be damned if I give up a man."

resolve the matter regarding Owen's murder and to report the conditions of the Creek territory to authorities in Washington. The case involving the Owen murder was eventually dropped, and indictments against the soldiers were dismissed. Key wrote a deposition regarding the condition of the Creek people and claimed that the hostile nature of white settlers had driven the crimes of retaliation. He also added that the depravities and neglect of the United States government had weakened the already poor conditions within the Indian territories, leaving the Indian populations defenseless against the new citizenry of the region.

While Key stayed at Fort Mitchell, he wrote often and is credited today for the lyrics of our national anthem, "The Star-Spangled Banner." But his reports of the awful tragedies happening in the Creek Nation were ignored in Washington, and the bad blood and war mongering between settlers and Indians grew even more fierce.

Villainy and crime in the Indian territories were growing substantially. Many of the Indians sought refuge in Sodom, even at the risk of becoming victims of its evil. It was the only means of safety available to them. The transgressions against the people of Girard had driven them further and further into blackness. It wouldn't be long before the region would collapse under an umbrella of criminal activity that would control the location for nearly one hundred years.

The Grave Robbers of Dog Scratch Hill

By 1836, the Creek people had been robbed of their ancestral lands and swindled out of government property by settlers and their own tribesmen. The Creek people could no longer trust the settlers or the government agents appointed to aid the transitions of landownership. As a result, many of the tribes in the Russell and Lee County regions began to hide caches of silver coins given to them as payment for their land by the United States government. The coins were often buried with their dead in tribal burial grounds. This is possibly the reason why many believe that Indian burial grounds are cursed or haunted. Indian superstition played a great part in diverting thieves from Indian graveyards, but not all of those superstitious tales would prevail.

According to accounts retold by early historians, a tribe of Lower Creeks, who once lived in the Beauregard community of Lee County, buried hundreds of pots of silver coins in the tribe's burial grounds. This particular burial site was located just east of the (Watoola) creek. Paddy Carr, the half-blood son of an Irishman and a Creek woman, was one of the many chiefs whose tribal dead were buried at the Watoola (Wataula) location. Paddy Carr's father was a merchant trader who came to America and settled near Fort Mitchell with the prominent Crowell family. Between 1817 and 1825, Fort Mitchell was an established community of commerce for the Indians. John Crowell was appointed agent to the Creeks at Fort Mitchell in 1821, and his brother Thomas ran the local tavern that would later become part of the officers' quarters. When Paddy's father returned to Ireland, he left his Creek wife and children in the care of John Crowell, but Carr never returned to retrieve them.

Paddy Carr was educated in white schools and learned math, English and how to read and write. He retained the culture of his mother and was fluent in both Muscogee and English. This later made him a valuable asset to the Crowell family, and he eventually became an interpreter. His maternal side hailed from the Lower Creek towns in what are today Russell and Lee Counties. Many of his forefathers were buried in the traditional mounds where the natives lived in east Alabama for hundreds of years. In these mounds, specifically near the Wataula Creek, is where the silver caches were rumored to be hidden.

Unlike some American Indian cultures, the Creek Indians buried their dead. Bodies were wrapped in shrouds and lowered into shallow graves. The bodies were then covered with long strips of bark. The bark was scraped from pen-poles (long trees typically used in building their living structures). When the bark was removed from the poles, it was laid on the ground and weighted with heavy stones until completely dry. These long strips of dried bark could repel wind and water and other debris for many years. This bark was used in burials to cover the body in the ground, and a layer of earth was placed on top of it.

Paddy Carr was a mixed-race Muscogee Indian whose mother was part of the Royal Wind Clan. The graves of some of his Indian ancestors were once located near the settlement of Watoola in what is today Lee County. Deposits of silver coins, given to the Indians by the government as payment for their lands, were buried in the Indian graveyard. Though plundered for many years, not all the treasure was found. *Courtesy of the Library of Congress.*

Important hunting items like tomahawks, bows and knives were placed inside the graves of Indian men. It was the same for the women, only their personal effects consisted of pot ware, dishes and household items they used most frequently. Days of mourning typically followed. Traditionally, the Creeks spent days crying over their dead. This was a sign of respect. The more important the person was, the longer the mourning and crying endured.

Paddy's relationship with his tribe wasn't always pleasant; in fact, many of his people viewed him as a traitor for siding with the government after the Creek revolt of 1836. But his apprehension of being stricken down by his own people didn't stop him from investigating the claims of silver coins buried in the graves of his forefathers. On his return to the Watoola burial grounds, he discovered that many of the burial sites of Creek chieftains had been violated and disturbed. There were other locations, of far more importance to him, that had also been dug up. Shards of pottery and empty pots lay scattered all over the burial site, but not one silver coin could be found.

According to Lee County's first historians, the rumor of the buried silver wasn't such a well-guarded secret. Settlers from all over the region came to the Watoola burial site to dig up the graves in search of the Indian treasure. It was later noted that certain families in the county hit a streak of good fortune. Because of the grave-robbing renegades, the location came to be called "Dog Scratch Hill." For many years after, the area was still pillaged for silver. It was noted by Paddy Carr and other important tribesmen that not all the caches were discovered.

Another account associated with this pillaged burial ground comes from an archived story regarding the Reverend James W. Capps. He moved to Russell County in 1837, just a few miles south of Opelika, to an area that is today Lee County. Conveniently, this homestead—on which he squatted briefly, was evicted from and then moved back to—was also within the same location of the Creek burial grounds, near Dog Scratch Hill. The reverend was a respected member of the neighborhood and was most recognized for building the first house of worship in the area: the Watoola Church.

In the year 1839, the Capps family property was settled by C.W. Dupree, and a reputable source shares the account of a grave that was unearthed on the Dupree settlement. Inside the grave was the rotting corpse of an Indian woman, along with several pieces of expensive china. The dishes would have been a very valuable possession to either Indian or settler, but according to the story, the grave wasn't disturbed further, and the corpse and its fine tableware were covered up and left alone. A few years later, an unnamed man who had seen the dishes in the grave of the Indian woman saw and recognized them on the table of a family who lived just ten miles from the Watoola burial ground.

Fancy a civilized man dining every day from plates which had lain an unknown period of time in the coffin, in close contact with the decaying corpse of an Indian squaw!
—Francis Lafayette Cherry

Golgotha Hill

Crawford, Alabama

Crawford, Alabama, is located just a few miles from Ladonia, just outside the Phenix City limits in Russell County. The small community hasn't changed much since its infancy in 1832, when it was settled and known as Crockettsville, named for the famous "king of the wild frontier" and Tennessee scout David "Davy" Crocket. The location served as the county seat for Russell County from 1839 until 1868. The federal road that ran through this portion of the county reached Montgomery and is sometimes referred to as the Old Montgomery Highway.

Crockettsville was a newly established town in 1842 with a courthouse located in the center of town, a jail, mercantile stores, homes and churches. In 1848, the Tuckabatchee Masonic Lodge was built across the street from the courthouse and is one of the only surviving landmarks form the community today. The town limits extended about a mile in every direction from the courthouse, which was built on the location where the Crawford United Methodist Church can be found today.

During the Civil War, the rural community was spared by Union forces after a female prisoner pleaded to Union general James Wilson not to burn the town. She professed that she had been imprisoned for her support of the Union and for an attempt to steal slaves. She was arrested in Girard and held in the jail until threats from an angry mob forced the sheriff to move her to Crockettsville. Wilson's Raiders burned the jail, but the rest of the town was spared, and the Union forces moved on to Girard.

The Crockettsville Courthouse handled the vast majority of trials and criminal cases that existed in the small southern territory. The shanty tent and front yard courts that had existed in Girard were now being held in Russell County's first courthouse. Because of the region's proximity to neighboring communities, an annex to the courthouse had to be built to handle the overflow of prisoners and court cases. The annex was built in Salem, which was then (and still is) an independent community in Lee County.

The Russell County annex is a two-story structure made of simple mortar and stone. The bottom floor, which was used as the courtroom during trials and for town business, consists of two large rooms connected by a single doorway, and a small passage of wooden steps lead upstairs to the prison cells. Salem resident and Confederate soldier Richard Floyd gave an account of his experience at the courthouse during a trial

Crawford, Alabama, is located outside Phenix City in Russell County. The community was established in 1832 and named Crockettsville after Davy Crocket, king of the wild frontier. *Courtesy of the Library of Congress.*

sometime in the mid-1840s. While Floyd was sitting in the jury popping parched peanuts, the judge looked up at the sheriff and said, "Mr. Sheriff, someone is popping peanuts. You find him and bring him to me. I'll have him put in jail for contempt of court." Mr. Floyd was certain not to pop another peanut in that courtroom.

As early as 1820, Alabama decided it would not have a prison system. Frontier people found that justice moved more swiftly under the law of local officals. Petty crimes for gambling or alcohol were often enforced with hefty fines and extensive jail time. Harsher offenses for murder, rape, fraud and theft of cattle or slaves would often result in executions. Public executions were expected during frontier times and were accepted as justice for serious crimes. Hanging was the most common form of execution; however, on occasion, some prisoners were shot. Located about a half mile from the original courthouse in Crockettsville is a grassy foothill named for the place of Jesus's crucifixion: Golgotha Hill.

Golgotha, in Hebrew, means "place of the skull," which essentially refers to the landscape of hills that resembles the top of a human skull. However, the metaphoric symbolism is far more sinister in nature. Executions were

The old hanging tree that once stood on Golgotha Hill is now part of privately owned property in Crawford, Alabama. It shares another historical location known to only a few locals as the "old moonshine trail."

carried out on Golgotha Hill in full view of the public. Families and children gathered to watch the condemned die. They held picnics and cheered as the prisoners stood on the gallows or waited as the hangman fashioned the noose.

The actual location of Golgotha Hill is now private property. Nature has taken over this hallowed ground and reclaimed it back into the earth. It's nearly a forgotten part of southeast Alabama's history, serving as a haunting reminder of those who have perished under the noose of justice in Crawford, Alabama.

III

THE BIRTH OF SIN CITY

Illegal and Economic Whiskey in Girard

In 1900, Alabama was seeking to establish and enforce liquor laws to prohibit the manufacturing and sale of illicit alcohol. Moralists rallied all over the state in order to gain support of prohibition, and groups such as the Woman's Christian Temperance Union and the Anti-Saloon Leagues worked together with preachers and politicians in order to rid Alabama of alcohol altogether.

By 1913, every candidate running for governor in Alabama supported the concept of a "bone-dry" state and zero tolerance for alcohol. This led to a massive increase in supporters of prohibition, and in 1914, those political figures were in control of the state legislature. In 1915, with the support of the moralist groups and communities rallying to do away with whiskey in Alabama, the state passed a law making the manufacture and sale of alcohol illegal two years before prohibition became national.

The whiskey business in Girard had been an economic staple in the community for several years. Whiskey warehouses and distilleries, totaling more than $300,000 in alcohol products, manufactured and distributed to outside states such as New York, Massachusetts (Boston) and Illinois (Chicago). Because the region was the farthest navigational point on the Chattahoochee River, alcohol distributors also shipped out their products by boat to Savannah, Georgia, and the coastal ports of South Carolina. Girard's distilleries were so big and the demand so high

Most of the South's earliest economic resources were retarded by the Civil War. The Eagle Phenix Mill served as a primary source of income for many rural families in Girard. Poverty grew in the mill communities due to low pay, lack of benefits, injury and accidental death. *Courtesy of the Library of Congress.*

that a Citizen's Bank had to be incorporated to handle the money and business transactions.

Though the state laws on prohibition made all these activities illegal by 1915, Girard depended on the industry in order to survive and opted to ignore prohibition laws and remain a wet county. Millworkers who lived in Girard made about nine dollars a week at the Eagle Phenix Mill. Alabama farmers were suffering statewide due to an infestation of boll weevils, which devoured the primary cash crop of cotton. It was virtually necessary for Girard to break the law for the purposes of maintaining its livelihood.

State organizations were formed to specifically monitor, enforce and control prohibition laws. These government groups of revenuers were deputized and legally bonded as lawmen of the day. Because Girard was openly manufacturing and bootlegging illegal alcohol, the criminal activity within the city reached an insurmountable level. Girard was considered the slum of Russell County. Only the lower life forms of society congregated there. This type of lawlessness didn't sit well with some citizens in Girard,

On May 17, 1916, a train carrying forty revenue agents from Montgomery traveled to Girard. The agents destroyed hundreds of gallons of whiskey in an effort to stop the manufacturing and sale of illicit alcohol in Girard. *Courtesy of the Library of Congress.*

and when the good people tried to interfere, homes and businesses were burned and their property destroyed. People were beaten and found with their throats cut, and some mysteriously vanished. All these offenses had state revenuers fixed on stopping the criminal activity in Girard.

On May 17, 1916, a train carrying forty revenuers from Montgomery came to the city at approximately 5:00 a.m. By mid-morning, they were armed and breaking down the doors at the whiskey warehouses and illegal establishments. A crowd of about one thousand spectators looked on as the owners were arrested and the whiskey barrels dragged into the streets and smashed open, sending gallons of hooch gushing down Dillingham Street.

By that afternoon, more than four thousand people had come to Girard to watch the destruction. The revenue agents carried barrel after barrel, bottle after bottle, of everything from beer and wine to gin and whiskey to Thompson's ditch behind the warehouse on Dillingham Street and dumped it out, creating a proverbial river of alcohol that flowed down into the Chattahoochee. Children and onlookers waded in the stream of liquor they called "whiskey creek."

Along with a number of other prominent community officials and leaders in Russell County, the sheriff in Girard, Pal. M. Daniel, was arrested in

In 1915, prohibition outlawed alcohol in Alabama. However, Girard chose to openly defy the laws and continued to manufacture and sell alcohol out of necessity. The alcohol industry was so prominent in Girard that a bank had to be opened for the sole purpose of handling the whiskey sales and transactions. *Courtesy of the Library of Congress.*

the raid of 1916 for possession of illegal liquor. The raid seemed to slow down the alcohol problem, but it certainly did not resolve it. Illegal sales and distilling continued, but in a stealthier manner, until about 1923, when Girard would receive another visit from Montgomery revenuers. Federal agents raided Girard again, destroying over one hundred gallons of liquor and manufacturing stills. In 1925, the manufacturing of watermelon beer brought the revenuers back once more, and in 1927, it was corn liquor and moonshine. By 1931, a dope ring of morphine dealers had been rounded up and arrested in Girard and taken to the state capitol to face drug charges.

After World War I, on the verge of the Great Depression, Girard was slowly getting back to what it knew: illegal and criminal activity. Camp Benning, located across the river in Georgia, made Girard off limits to soldiers who found the city too enticing to avoid. Gambling, prostitution and alcohol seemed to make for a good time until soldiers visiting any of the city's clip joints complained about the loaded dice, shady hookers and watered-down alcohol. They were typically taken outside and beat up or cut up or tossed in the river through trapdoors in the back of the clubs.

Sometimes charges were filed against the criminals and establishment owners, but few were ever arrested or sent to trial. Vice and immoral behavior were just part of what Girard offered its customers. The satisfaction of a good time was shadowed by the blackness of sin that was slowly consuming the city like a plague.

Poverty and the Vice Districts

With the frontier days behind them and the Civil War over, the settlements within the states of Alabama and Georgia began to flourish. Small villages grew into towns, and the towns grew into counties, annexing the smaller communities and growing the population. In the towns of Brownville and Girard, the populations had grown to over 4,000 by 1900. When Phenix City was consolidated on August 9, 1923, it included the surrounding towns of Girard and Brownsville, bringing the population of the city to a staggering 10,374 people.

The Eagle Phenix Mill, located in Columbus, Georgia, was built in 1851 for milling cotton. It was the second-largest textile mill in Georgia during the Civil War until it was burned by Union forces. In 1869, the mill was rebuilt and continued to expand, nearly quadrupling in size. The work population

Poverty devastated many families living in the rural South after the Civil War. In Russell County, Alabama, 73 percent of the farming workforce was made up of African American sharecroppers. *Courtesy of the Library of Congress.*

from the communities in and around Phenix City was made up of a majority of white men. They composed 90 percent of the mill's workforce, leaving most of the sharecropping jobs to African Americans. Black farmers made up 73 percent of the farming community in Russell County.

Immigration also played a substantial role in the growing populations in Russell County. Immigrants came to the region and opened distilleries, butcher shops and stores. Carl Willaeur and Earnest Koenueker, both of German descent, built a two-story, Bavarian-style brewery in 1888 on Crawford Road called the Chattahoochee Brewing Company. Their thriving brewery was noted for its brewing tanks, made from cypress trees found in the Chattahoochee River. They also made their own kegs from white oak found in the Uchee Swamp. Both men were master brewers, and their establishment turned out nearly fifty barrels of corn-based beer a day, making the Chattahoochee Brewing Company one of the largest legal breweries in Russell County.

Most of Phenix City was still dirt roads and small, shanty mill villages in 1900. Fourteenth Street was known as Vinegar Hill then and was the sprawling business district of the city. It was typically crowded with merchants and stores. But some of the city's earliest gambling houses could also be found here alongside legal distillers. Card houses, with shady dealers, lured in unsuspecting players. For a small sum, you could buy your hand into a game of poker or faro, betting all you could afford and getting cheated out of a week's pay. Other games, such as "street craps" or dice, were more common. Players would bet on the outcome of a series of rolls in order to win. Often, loaded dice (dice weighted or rigged to land on certain numbers every time) were used to fool the unsuspecting players, resulting in unbeatable odds.

Small saloons where homemade liquor was sold and often traded dotted the river's edge. It was almost completely necessary for the small city to depend on these types of enterprises to bring in revenue for schools, businesses and even churches. The activity throughout the turn of the century in Phenix City may have been morally corrupt, but it did provide the town with a way to build an economy.

In 1918, just after the First World War, the United States School for Infantry training was moved from Fort Sill, Oklahoma, to just outside Columbus, Georgia. The first troops to arrive at Camp Benning came on October 5, 1918. Approximately 367 men from Fort Sill marched to a location near the Wynnton area and began working to set up camp the following day. In 1919, the camp was moved to a permanent location, nine miles outside Columbus. The main post area consisted of mostly tents where enlisted men lived but also some small houses where officers lived and buildings where they worked. By the early 1920s, Fort Benning had acquired more than nine thousand acres of land for its building and training facilities. This brought the base population to over 7,000 troops: 350 officers and 650 military student officers. Recreational facilities were built at Benning and included football and baseball stadiums, swimming pools and a theater.

Fort Benning's proximity to Phenix City also gave it another economic resource in soldiers. Men stationed at Benning would travel across the Chattahoochee River whenever they could. However, the recreations of Phenix City were far different from those found on base. Some of the city's old habits never died out, and gambling, liquor and women drove the soldiers to come to Phenix City often.

Over the next thirty years, Alabama's established laws to eradicate alcohol would play a substantial part in the economy of Phenix City, as well as shape its personality. It would grow from the rural, southern town whose growth was retarded by the Civil War to an urbanized region of Alabama. In the

During the Great Depression, economic collapse struck all Alabama farmers. Families of all races found themselves sharing the same problems, and cotton farming communities were almost wiped out due to the infestations of boll weevils sweeping across the South. *Courtesy of the Library of Congress.*

shadow of the mill industry, poor and destitute families were struggling to put food on the table. Pay was considerably low, and jobs were extremely scarce. For every one man who was employed at the mills, a dozen or more waited for jobs.

During the Great Depression, the state of Alabama suffered immensely. No community was hit harder than that of the African American farmers and sharecroppers in Alabama. Jobs were few, and poverty was high, leaving many Americans to seek out employment anywhere they could. African Americans, who had been restricted to domestic jobs and hard farm labor, were now sharing the unemployment line with poor white men and women seeking the same employment, making blue-collar jobs even harder to come by.

In 1940, Phenix City citizens were in a state of dire straits. That year, the Federal Housing Authority built and opened the projects at Riverview Apartments to poor whites. The following year, the Fredrick Douglas Homes were opened to blacks, making Phenix City, Alabama, the only city in the state with a population of fifteen thousand that had two federal housing projects. Even by today's standards, the locations would have been seen as ghettos. Only the poorest and most deprived of the community lived there. Poverty stricken and desperate, many Phenix City residents turned to crime as a way to survive. The city was socially crippled and morally corrupt, and criminal entrepreneurs who would build on the enterprise of sin found Phenix City to be the perfect breeding ground for their exploits.

The Business of Gambling

Aside from the loaded dice and shady card players of Girard Village, a more regal and aspiring community of gamblers had made its way through the ranks of Phenix City's underworld. These men formed some organizations within the city that appealed not only to deep-pocket gamblers but also to some of the general public.

Hoyt Shepherd was born in Alabama in 1899 but was raised in LaGrange, Georgia. After losing his mill job, he moved to Phenix City and met English-born Jimmy Matthews. Shepherd and Matthews together were known as the S&M Syndicate. They supplied the majority of rigged gambling equipment to the vice districts of Phenix City. Gambling equipment such as marked cards, loaded dice and rigged roulette wheels and slot machines were just a few of the products they offered. In return for tax revenues, they offered licenses to set up gambling casinos on the Chattahoochee River.

In 1938, a lottery organized by the S&M Syndicate known as "The Bug" swept through Phenix City, drawing disadvantaged and poor millworkers by the hundreds. The lottery took place at the Ritz Café, located on Dillingham Street, and millworkers flocked to the location for their chance to hit the big bucks. On April 20, 1938, an enormous crowd gathered inside the café. While they were waiting for the winning numbers to be announced, a section of the roof collapsed onto the crowd, leaving ten people injured. The following day, twice as many people shoved and pushed into the club, and a load-bearing wall collapsed, killing twenty-four people and injuring eighty-three more. The families of those who were killed demanded that a lawsuit be filed against Shepherd and Matthews and their colleague, Clyde Yarbrough, but it never made it to court.

Within the gambling organizations, there existed a separate crime family of equally lawless men and women who also played crucial roles in the criminal

In 1952, a federal law mandated that all gambling establishments had to be registered for tax purposes. In Alabama, 270 registrations were sent out to gambling houses; 230 of them were in Phenix City.

empires of Phenix City. Horace "Pat" Webster ran the Phenix City Card Company, which was located on Long Street. He rigged everything, from slot machines to marked cards that he ordered from wholesale companies in Chicago and Los Angeles. He also outfitted equipment for other crooked organizations in surrounding states. By 1952, a federal law had been passed that required all gambling establishments to be registered for tax purposes and identification. In Alabama, 270 registrations went out, and 230 of them were in Phenix City.

Loan sharking, extortion, bribery, prostitution, drugs, illegal alcohol and even a community of common thieves gathered in what was quickly being labeled the "Wickedest City in America." Phenix City offered no fewer than seventeen clubs on or east of Fourteenth Street, near Dillingham Street. Some of those clubs were Yarbrough's Café, owned by Clyde Yarbrough; Riverside Café, owned by Glenn Youngblood; and the Ritz Café and 602 Club (located behind the Ritz Café), both owned by A.B. "Buck" Billingsley. The Silver Slipper, Manhattan Café and Manhattan Club were all owned by Davis Enterprises. The Silver Dollar, Yellow Front Café, New Bridge Café, the Hi-Lo Club, Curt's Café, the Blue Goose, Bennies Café and the Blue Bonnet Café were all located inside city limits. Perhaps the biggest, and

In the 1950s, anyone looking for a good time in Phenix City could find card houses, gambling, beer joints and strip clubs up and down Fourteenth Street.

allegedly the straightest, out of all the vice district gambling houses was the infamous BAMA Club, owned by Hoyt Shepherd and Jimmy Matthews.

There were several small groceries and stores in Phenix City that also offered gambling of some sort. Girard Cleaners, along with Original Barbecue, owned by Red Cook, offered lotteries. The Bridge Grocery, co-owned by C.O. "Head" Revel and George Davis Sr., was the Metropolitan Lottery headquarters. The grocery store also offered slots, dice, poker and roulette. In some stores, stools were placed at the counters for children. This encouraged even the very young to gamble their milk money on rigged slots and faulty gaming machinery.

Other clubs were located just outside the city but offered many of the same amenities. These clubs and cafés were located near Highway 431 (toward Seale) and on Highway 80, heading toward Crawford. Those clubs were Jacks Café, the Hi-Way Tavern, Red Top Café and the Bamboo Club, which was considered one of the finest establishments outside the city. A few clubs were also strictly "colored." They were Club Avalon, located at 1500 Seale Road, and the New York Club, located at 1648 Fountain Road. The Cotton Club, owned by the "Queen of Hearts," Fannie Bell Chance, was also among the swing houses and strip clubs surrounding Phenix City.

The gambling enterprise in Phenix City was a force almost completely unchallenged. However, this all changed for Hoyt Shepherd in 1946, when he and his brother were indicted for the murder of Fate Leebern, a Columbus resident and avid gambler. Hoyt Shepherd hired Phenix City lawyer Albert Patterson, along with every other available attorney in town. Grady, Hoyt's brother, was arrested for the murder but was later found innocent on the grounds of self-defense. In 1952, town organizations like the Russell County Betterment Association were bearing down on the syndicate groups in Phenix City. Shepherd never did any extended time for his part as a syndicate leader. Ultimately, he invested his money into political campaigns and some legitimate businesses. He also donated to churches and schools, wanting to make a better name for himself and his family in the community.

Working Girls

Among the nightclubs, dance halls and gambling houses in Phenix City, there existed another deplorable form of sin and vice: prostitution. For what it's worth, prostitution is the oldest profession in history. The exchange of sex for money or other personal gain has been an enterprising way of doing business since the days of the Roman Empire. However, the whorehouses and strip clubs of Phenix City were not among the classy joints of the swing era, and the horror stories of sex slaves, abortions, babies being sold, abuse and murder accompany this part of Alabama's history—a part most would prefer to forget altogether. However, there are a few stories from this era in Phenix City that are tastelessly humorous and a bit awkward as well.

Ma Beachie's

Anytime I hear the name "Ma Beachie," I think back to a story my grandmother told me many years ago. It was around 1954 when she and a girlfriend took a taxi from Fort Benning, Georgia, over the Chattahoochee River, accompanied by two friendly soldiers, to Phenix City. The atmosphere was exciting, and neon signs lit up the whole town at dark. As they reached their destination, they got out and walked up and down the main strip in town. Then they left the busy district for a small club they heard was located just a short distance away.

My grandmother said she had absolutely no idea what kind of club they were walking into. But that didn't seem relevant since they were just going to have a few drinks with these nice Fort Benning soldiers. Once they entered the club, she and her girlfriend felt a little awkward since they seemed to be overshadowed by several scantily dressed women. So to be polite, they agreed to have one drink with the soldiers and leave. It was obvious at this point that the place wasn't necessarily a "nice" place to hang out.

As they ordered their drinks, one of the women in the club came over to their table and asked to sit down. My grandmother replied, "Yes," and the woman continued to make small talk with them. As the conversation continued, the woman said to my grandmother, "You certainly are a lovely young lady, and I bet you could make a lot of money working here. How would you like a job?" My grandmother, being from a Christian upbringing, was not entirely naïve to the suggestion and politely turned her down. "No ma'am," she said. "I don't think my mama and daddy would approve of me working in a place like this." "That's too bad," said the woman. "There's a lot of money to be made here." And she excused herself from the table. When they left the bar, Grandma looked back at the club and read the sign

Women who worked in the strip clubs and clip joints in Phenix City, Alabama, were often referred to as "B-girls." Their job was to get customers, especially soldiers from Fort Benning, drunk enough to lose everything from their pants to what was in their pockets.

overhead. "Ma Beachie's," she said. "Well, that's one place I won't be going back to."

Inside the gambling and card houses, there existed an underground network of prostitution within the nightclubs and cafés of Phenix City. But they weren't always discrete. Pimps would often chauffer their ladies up and down the busy streets of the business district in the back of pickup trucks, flagging down soldiers and drunks for a ride and a "good time." They'd stop at one end of the street, pick up a paying customer who would get into the back with one of the harlots and drive up the street while they handled business in the back. They would drop off the customer at the end of the next street and pick up another for another shrewd transaction, repeating the process from dusk till dawn, up and down the street.

This sort of brazen and outward display of sex wasn't limited anywhere in or out of the city. It was often noted that couples engaged in the full throes of passion in café booths, behind half-closed curtains in nightclubs and even in dirty bathroom stalls. Phenix City's strip joints were among the worst around, and soldiers were often targeted by pimps and even the B-girls themselves. "B-girl" was a term that referred to the women and girls who worked in the strip clubs and clip joints. Their job was to get men drunk enough to lose everything from their pants to what was in their pockets.

Ma Beachie's place was a little different. It was considered "soldier friendly," and if the word "classy" could be used when referring to a strip club, Ma Beachie's was it. It didn't, however, keep the fellas from losing their pants or anything in them. Ma Beachie herself would often hold on to money for drunk soldiers. She even placed little notes inside their pockets, letting them know how much money they came in with, how much they spent and what they went home with. This grandmotherly woman of the Sin City era of Phenix City pleaded ignorance to what was happening in her club during the cleanup of the city, but she did what she had to do to make a living.

Ma Beachie lost her first husband at thirty-four and later remarried and moved to New Orleans, where she was introduced to the nightclubs and saloons of the Big Easy. When she returned to Alabama, she brought with her the concepts and ideas of a New Orleans nightclub, and on July 14, 1937, she set up her own. The floor shows offered the best and most talented strippers in town. Not to mention, Ma Beachie wouldn't allow just any woman to bare herself in her club. Only the prettiest dolls worked at Ma Beachie's.

After the cleanup and lockdown of Phenix City clubs, Ma was arrested, but the charges were later dismissed, and she continued working. Instead of serving up strippers, she was serving up suppers. The reality of her enterprise being taken away didn't waver her spirit, and she continued on, caring for her children and grandchildren and working within the confines of the law for many years until her death.

The Queen of Hearts

In 1953, the number of strip clubs in Phenix City was astounding. Both inside and outside the city limits, anyone looking for a good time could find it and, often, a whole lot more. B-girls lured men into the clubs with the promise of a good time, making them spend as much money as they could. Soldiers were particularly vulnerable and among the worst treated in these types of establishments. The girls were required by state law to provide adequate information regarding their age, but this was not the case on the Phenix City level. Girls as young as twelve reportedly worked in these establishments. No regulations from the proprietors of the clubs were ever expected. In fact, some of the owners preferred to employ young girls over women, enslaving them with fear and capitalizing on their broken innocence.

Some of the women working in the endless strip clubs and prostitution houses of Phenix City were even required to be tattooed as a sign of ownership. The Blue Bonnet Café offered gambling and prostitution. Frank Gullatt, who owned the Blue Bonnet, had his girls tattooed on the inside of their lips. This prevented them from running away, as well as from getting work elsewhere. When new girls showed up at a club for employment, the first place the club's owners looked was inside their lips. If they belonged to another pimp, they were thrown out.

The entertainment districts were almost too tempting for soldiers and tourists to turn down. Fighting men with a month's pay at a time often spent their entire wages with some persuasive encouragement from the B-girls. The club girls made a 50 percent commission on drinks bought for them. Bartenders put just enough liquor on top of the drinks to fool a customer into believing he was getting his money's worth. The average drink ran about ten dollars. Bartenders kept tallies on the drinks or bottles of champagne that were purchased for the girls. Recycling watered-down whiskey and alcohol was done for the purpose of saving volume but gaining a buck. It was also a common practice for bartenders to take unfinished drinks and pour them back into the bottle. When soldiers brought in their own liquor, the girls would pour themselves a huge glass and take it back to the bar. The bartender would then pour it into a bottle and resell it to customers.

On paydays, the clubs would literally be overflowing with Fort Benning soldiers. Over one hundred drinks a night would be purchased for the girls, who often never drank them but playfully spilled them on the floor and asked for another. Customers, stricken by the idea of "getting lucky," eagerly obliged their B-girl waitresses. Girls weren't just acting as manipulative hostesses for drunken soldiers. When the fellas got too liquored up to stand or drunk enough to complain about the liquor, they, along with muscle-bound doormen (hired to look out for the club's best interest), took them outside and beat the daylights out of them. Whatever money, jewelry, cigarettes or other items of value they found on a helpless victim, they took before leaving him crippled and spitting out teeth.

The deprived woman who worked in these clubs were often victims of circumstance, but a few came to Phenix City for the purpose of making a living. One of those aspiring young women was Fannie Belle Chance. She moved to Phenix City from Corinth, Mississippi, and started out as a B-girl working in local clubs around Phenix City. She was making about fourteen dollars a week as she bounced from club to club, working in whatever profession was required of her. She managed to support herself in this way for several years and even married six different men in the process. It's unclear whether she was ever legally married to all six men since some of them were married to her at the same time. One of her soldier boys purchased her a fine home in Columbus, Georgia, while others supplied her with savings bonds and other money they sent to her to cover her living expenses. She made a substantial living from her military husbands, who paid her in allotments while they were overseas. All the while, they were under the impression that she was a faithful wife and girlfriend.

One of Fannie's boyfriends was the Phenix City chief of police, Buddy Jowers. Jowers was reportedly a huge man, over six feet tall, who typically smoked an equally large cigar. Fannie and Buddy ran a gambling and strip club together called the Cotton Club. It was one of the most recognized whorehouses in Phenix City, and Jowers's connections to the Phenix City deputy sheriff, Albert Fuller, kept the prostitution and underground sex slaves from prying eyes. Albert Fuller frequently extorted the clubs for money. He visited Cliff Entrekin's Fish Camp three times a week to collect his dues. Cliff's Fish Camp was located just outside town, on Highway 80, and along with rigged slot machines, it was reportedly the largest whorehouse in the county. Oddly, locals said the Fish Camp restaurant had the best fried fish in town.

With Deputy Fuller's cuts of the strip clubs in exchange for his silence, along with Jowers's protection from the law, Fannie Belle provided the entertainment at the Cotton Club, with no worries of consequences for breaking the law. According to the testimonies and reports of several woman who worked in the sex industries of the city, there existed another branch of prostitution—a tragedy in itself and one that has scarred the face of Russell County for an eternity.

The Kidnapping of Shelia Ann Harper

Earlene Harper came to Phenix City in 1952 with a few friends. The day she arrived, she and her friends were arrested and kept in jail for several days. According to her story, there was no reason for the arrest. This was a ploy used by crooked law enforcement officers in Phenix City to force women into prostitution or to work for the cafés and clubs that kept them as virtual slaves.

Earlene was one of the lucky ones. She was released by the Phenix City police after the FBI got suspicious of her and her friends' arrest. However, she was constantly hounded by a local pimp and club owner named Glenn Youngblood. Youngblood and his brother, Earnest, owned several cafés and clubs in Phenix City. On several occasions, Earlene was asked to work for Yongblood. She denied him until she was forced to accept his offer when the police said they would arrest her again, this time for vagrancy, if she didn't find a job. At that point, she started working for Youngblood at the Riverside Café. The café was a gambling house and oyster bar, with a loan company (also owned by Youngblood) next door.

Earlene was a B-girl in the clubs, but because of her status, she took her sixteen-year-old daughter, Shelia Ann, with her. Shelia made a habit of carrying a notebook everywhere she went. When she accompanied her mother to work, she wrote in it like a journal and documented the things she heard and saw in the clubs. Earnest Youngblood had Shelia drive him home often. Typically, he was too drunk to drive, but there was another reason Youngblood was after Shelia. Just like her mother, Youngblood hounded her to work for him in the club. Shelia refused him, and when she retorted with the fact that she was only sixteen, he told her it didn't matter. There were girls working for him who were much younger than she was.

Shelia mentioned on one of her trips to Earnest Youngblood's house, she was asked to retrieve some log books. The records that Youngblood kept were of the girls and women he employed as prostitutes and B-girls at his clubs. A small library of about five books, with hundreds of names and information regarding each woman, were categorized and filed away in years of records and notes. When Shelia attempted to leave Youngblood's house, he refused to let her go. She called the police, but since they were in on the prostitution ring in Phenix City, they never came to help her. Shelia threatened him with the information she had in her journals, and he reluctantly let her go.

This would prove to be a wise but dangerous mistake for Shelia. Earnest Youngblood's bartender was a man named Hugh Kinnard. He and his wife, Jean, kidnapped Shelia and left for South Carolina when the FBI started to look more closely into the events and tragedies that were happening in Phenix City. Shelia was able to get a letter to her mother regarding her whereabouts. Two days after she was taken, the Aiken, South Carolina police located the girl and returned her to Phenix City. She was kept in military custody pending the investigation of the Phenix City syndicates.

The Kinnards knew that the heat was on in Phenix City. Martial law had been enforced at this time, and state officials were determined to put a stop to all the crime and vice that had been going on in Russell County for decades. The Kinnards' involvement in the prostitution ring and kidnapping would surely get them both lengthy prison sentences. There were more girls besides Shelia who were taken. An undetermined number of female sex slaves were taken from Phenix City with the intent of setting up a similar industry at Fort Gordon for soldiers and the numerous millworkers in Aiken.

The cases of prostitution, sexual abuse, enslavement, gross misconduct and other horrible crimes were stacking up in Phenix City. The devastation of the underworld was just starting to reach the surface. According to court documents and testimonies, a local woman and retired madam named Louise Malinosky testified to her part in the prostitution ring. She admitted in court that she had performed abortions for women who found themselves pregnant with unwanted children. She apparently conducted the horrible surgical procedures on her kitchen table. Mrs. Malinosky said in her defense, "I did it to get pin money for whiskey and to help those poor girls in trouble." Louise was an alcoholic and washed-up rabbit farmer whose husband claimed he had no idea that such terrible things were going on in his home.

Other rumors of baby sales came to light after her testimony as well. Local attorney Albert Patterson defended a seventeen-year-old girl from Phenix City who was forced into prostitution. Instead of choosing to

In 1952, some staff and local doctors at Cobb Hospital were allegedly involved in an underground baby market. Infants were being sold to childless couples all over the United States. These allegations surfaced when a young woman from Phenix City hired attorney Albert Patterson in an effort to find her son, who was taken shortly after birth at Cobb.

terminate her pregnancy, she met with a doctor and county case worker at Cobb Hospital who told her she could give her baby up for adoption. When she had her baby, she was forced to sign documents and hand him over to the hospital staff. Once she changed her mind, she was no longer able to locate the paperwork or the adopted parents or get any legal help from local authorities to find her son. Selling babies in Phenix City wasn't just another horrible circumstance; it was a shadowy business from which city officials were making tons of money. Just like everything else in Phenix City, even children came with a price tag.

IV

CRIME AND CORRUPTION

The Phenix City Machine

Over the course of about two hundred years after the conception and birth of "Sin City," it was ultimately growing into a place of nefarious evil. The corruption and vice in the city divided communities into God-fearing and wicked citizens. The beautiful riverfront town was now covered in a shroud of unholy blackness and sin. It seemed the good people who lived in and around Phenix City were, at least in the beginning, naïve to the things that were happening behind the slum bar doors and in underground organizations. No more foul or detestable place existed in the American South than Phenix City during this time. It was compared to other cities with some of the worst criminal enterprises in the nation: Chicago, Boston, New York and Atlantic City. Big-name mob bosses and crime lords like Mickey Cohen, Frank Costello, Charles "Lucky" Luciano and Carlo Bambino weren't part of the headlines in southeast Alabama. It seemed the major syndicates of America were kept at a distance, from what the public could tell. But in the Phenix City underworld, a machine was progressing, evolving into a monster so fierce that it would eventually plunge every resident of Russell County into chaos and mayhem.

The opposition in Phenix City was outnumbered and outmatched. By the 1950s, the wicked people who organized and capitalized on the corruption within the branches of law enforcement and political offices gained absolute control over the city and all the vice districts. Lawyers, policemen, deputies and politicians were all kept on criminal payrolls in order to keep the Dixie Mafia running smoothly. There was simply nothing that could stop them; no force would dare stand up against such a powerhouse of criminal enterprise. Citizens were eventually forced to recognize the mob presence in Phenix City. All over the county, they were beginning to feel the effects and the harsh reality that controlled the city from the inside out. Phenix City had become a festering sore, a blemish and disgrace to the state of Alabama.

Hoyt Shepherd and the Murder of Fate Leebern

Hoyt Shepherd built his gambling empire in Phenix City along with his friend and colleague Jimmy Matthews starting in the early 1940s. Shepherd may have started out in Phenix City as a simple criminal, scamming local card games and rigging slot machines, but his involvement in the underworld syndicates propagated over time. During the time he was involved with the Phenix City machine, Shepherd was part of a number of crimes. Racketeering and murder were among the most noted, but his ability to hire every lawyer in town, pay off police and buy out local judges often resulted in charges being dropped. Though his best efforts were made later in life to remove the stigma he had placed on himself as a mob kingpin, the crimes he committed against Phenix City and his involvement in political scams and vice will probably never be dismissed.

Shepherd's involvement in the murder of Columbus gangster Lafayette Leebern came after he helped rig a local election in September 1946. He helped finance the campaign for city council, backing Elmer Reese, a strung-out politician who was on Shepherd's pay roll. Votes for Reese came in the form of purchased ballots, tombstone votes (ballots cast with the names of deceased individuals) and even a blind man who was brought down by Shepherd's cronies in the police department to cast his vote five times.

After Elmer Reese's landslide victory, Shepherd and his men celebrated at a local bar, the Southern Manor nightclub. While there, Shepherd noticed an old adversary from his liquor-running days, Lafayette "Fate" Leebern. Some years before, Shepherd and Leebern had faced off over territory and claims to the region's liquor districts. It was during that time that Shepherd told Leebern to stay away from Phenix City and threatened to kill him if he ever set foot in Alabama again. This kept Leebern on the Georgia side of the river for some time, but apparently his bravery and inability to stay

Hoyt Shepherd was considered the kingpin of the Dixie mafia in Phenix City. His involvement in racketeering, political scandals, gambling and even murder made him an infamous gangster. Later in life, Shepherd made an effort to remove the stigma by getting involved in legitimate businesses and contributing funds to local schools, churches and charities.

away from Phenix City's nightclubs were too much. Leebern had made a name for himself in Columbus, Georgia, as the owner of a wine and liquor distribution outfit. After prohibition, the first carload of legal alcohol in Columbus was offloaded at the Columbus Wine Company Distributors, owned by Leebern. He later tried to turn around his criminal life when he got involved in more legitimate businesses, making him a very wealthy man.

As Leebern sat at the table with his young companion, a beautiful nineteen-year-old blond woman from Columbus named Edna Roye, Hoyt and his brother, Grady, noticed the couple and began a terrible plot. Hoyt motioned for his brother, whose nickname was "Snooks," to head for the dice room in the back. Hoyt pulled out a pistol and a roll of money and placed it on the table in front of the club hostess. He handed her a twenty-dollar bill and told her, "Go buy yourself a pair of stockings." Snooks encouraged her to leave, and Hoyt told the bar manager to take a hike.

The men then approached Fate and asked him to join them in the dice room. Fate obliged them, but when they reached the door, Hoyt turned on him, and shots rang out in the club. The hostess hadn't even made it outside when she heard the thump of Leebern's body hitting the floor. He took two shots to the chest, killing him almost instantly. His lifeless body collapsed onto the floor, spilling blood from open wounds. Just as the crowded club began to realize what was happening, Snooks stood in the doorway of the dice room, folded his arms in front of his chest and said, "There's been some trouble. Somebody call the police."

The investigation of Fate Leebern's murder didn't last very long. Grady took the heat for the murder and was arrested. He claimed that he had killed Leebern in self-defense, saying that Fate came at him with a knife. A small and rather insignificant scratch was found on Grady's chest, where he claimed to have been attacked. Witnesses to the event, Jeanette Mercer, the hostess, and Otis Stewart, the bar floor manager, both mysteriously disappeared, leaving no trace of where they'd gone. Edna Roye was emotionally wrecked by Fate's murder. Her father would not allow her to speak with the press or give any sworn statement to the authorities because of the potential danger it posed.

The remaining witnesses to the murder were only Hoyt Shepherd and Jimmy Matthews, who both validated Snook's story of being attacked by Leebern. With the consensus of self-defense, four days after the murder, Grady Shepherd walked into city hall for a hearing. His attorney waived the preliminary in order for the case to go before a grand jury. A week into the investigation, Hoyt Shepherd and Jimmy Matthews were also arrested and charged with the murder of Fate Leebern. Hoyt hired every lawyer in town and one from the neighboring city of Opelika. The attorneys were Roy Smith, who was also Grady's attorney; Jabe Brassell; William Belcher; Julius Hicks; Arch Ferrell; and Albert Patterson.

A heated and lengthy trial went on for some time, but eventually Hoyt, Grady and Jimmy Matthews were all acquitted. A few of Shepherd's defense lawyers were genuinely disgusted at the idea of defending the men involved in Leebern's murder. However, one of those men would face off with the Phenix City machine again in what was, and still is, Phenix City's most infamous murder of all time.

Albert Fuller: Deadly Desperado

Albert Fuller grew up in Phenix City, Alabama, and attended Central High School. When he graduated, he drove a delivery bread truck until he joined the navy just before World War II. Fuller spent much of his navy career stationed in Texas, where he worked for the shore patrol and learned to shoot. He quickly became a gunslinger, much like those of the old Wild West. Fuller carried two gold-plated pistols in hip holsters and fashioned himself in semi-western attire, complete with a white Stetson hat and cowboy boots. He may have wanted to look the part of a desperado, but his activities and involvement in the criminal underground and corruption within the ranks of law enforcement made him more like the outlaw bandits who sought blood over glory.

Fuller got a job as a deputy with the Russell County Sheriff's Department in the early 1940s. His reputation as an "outlaw deputy" definitely fit his attitude, but it shadowed his privilege to serve and protect the people of Russell County and Phenix City. He extorted many of the club owners for money and was heavily involved in the prostitution rings that were part of a repetitive and vicious cycle he promoted. When young women came into Phenix City looking for work in the club districts, Deputy Fuller would arrest them on bogus charges for prostitution and then let the pimps from local clubs come down and offer to bail them out in exchange for the very service for which they were arrested. He was also a notorious stalker of young women. He would venture out into the country in search of young farm girls. Flashing his police badge and a wad of cash, he lured the naïve young women into town with money and promises of work, which they typically found in the whorehouses.

Fuller got paid to look the other way when criminal activity was taking place in the vice districts. He also provided the presence of law enforcement to deter state and federal officials from finding out what kind of improper activities were really going on in the clubs and cafés. He collected a quarter to 50 percent of the establishments' earnings in return for his services. Fuller worked under the not-so-watchful eye of Sheriff Ralph Matthews. Sheriff Matthews was a heavyset, pale man with an apathetic and unconcerned perspective toward his job and authority over the city. He worked for the Dixie mafia lords who ran the town like a western rodeo, and his prize bull was Deputy Albert Fuller.

When someone made a fuss in the city over any of the vice districts or syndicate organizations, Fuller was sent to rough them up. He was frequently

Albert Fuller was the bulldog deputy of Russell County who was responsible for a number of crimes, including extortion, prostitution and murder. It was rumored that he could "shoot the high heel off a whore from fifty yards."

to blame for the beatings of inmates in jail. He once pushed a taxi driver down a flight of stairs just because he was having a bad day. Fuller's fast guns and intimidating personality also hindered him within the ranks of mafia royalty, leaving him as the grunt labor and excluding him from the brains of the operation, where he preferred to be.

In 1949, Fuller was granted authority over every district in Russell County and Phenix City when he was appointed chief deputy sheriff. At the time, a liquor war between Alabama and Georgia had reached a critical point. Georgia revenuers were facing some serious opposition from Phenix City, which was being used as a safe ground in order to shield the rumrunners from the long arm of Georgia law enforcement. Georgia revenuers who were put in charge of ending bootlegging operations were sent down to watch for suspected whiskey runners and follow them until they crossed the state line. Once they returned to Georgia, they arrested the suspects and hauled them off to jail in Muscogee County. But the plan and efforts to stop the illegal liquor trade didn't go as planned. Approximately 20 percent of Phenix City's revenue depended on the bootlegging operation, and Phenix City mayor Homer Cobb (also a longtime resident and former millworker) said, "As I see it, the law officers arresting citizens in Georgia for purchasing liquor in Phenix City are violating the fundamentals of the Bill of Rights itself by depriving citizens of their property without due process of law."

Mayor Cobb sent down an order to Sheriff Matthews and the chief of police, Pal Daniel, to arrest anyone in Phenix City who was even suspected of working with the Georgia revenuers to stop the bootlegging operations. Georgia agents, in plain clothes, walked around the red-light districts of Phenix City, writing down tag numbers and looking for evidence regarding the identities of the whiskey runners. Two of those Georgia agents, E.E. Satterfield and Elzie Hancock, were arrested and put in jail in Phenix City on loitering charges. They were later released, and a federal agent with unlimited jurisdiction was appointed to handle the situation with his Georgia colleagues.

Federal agent Grady Cook took over the investigation of Guy and Pete Hargett, two brothers who were making a huge profit from running liquor over state lines. Cook met with Albert Fuller and the city ABC officer, Ben Scroggins, to raid the Hargett place and attempt to apprehend the suspects. Fuller knew if Hargett was taken alive, he would surely let the federal agents know about the city's involvement in harboring the whiskey runners. When they arrived at the house, the Georgia agents and Cook took a position around the back, while Fuller and Scroggins kicked in the front door. With guns drawn and no intention of letting the Hargett brothers leave alive, Albert Fuller unloaded on Guy while he sat in his chair. Guy Hargett's wife told police that he was asleep when Fuller came through the door and emptied his pistol into his chest and abdomen, leaving a line of bullet holes from his forehead to his belt buckle. Fuller alleged that Hargett drew a gun on him, so he acted in self-defense. Pete Hargett and a third man, Sam Beck, were arrested and sent to jail for assault and interfering with an investigation.

Fuller's time as a sheriff in Phenix City would leave behind him a trail of devastation and murder. His job should have been to serve and protect, but instead, he chose to neglect and destroy.

The Florida Body Dump

People involved in criminal activity in Phenix City during the late 1940s, both innocent and guilty, often came up missing. When criminal cases reached the point of trial, key witnesses would often disappear. Some left on their own, but others were taken. If those who left on their own were ever found, it was typically decades after a substantial criminal case or high-profile trial was closed. Others weren't so lucky; when those people resurfaced, it was because someone had uncovered their shallow graves or the waters of the Okefenokee Swamp, located on the edge of the Florida-Georgia line, had receded enough to recover human skeletons.

In 1944, three local hoods and known gamblers, Godwin Davis, Head Revel and Joe Allred, were arrested on liquor conspiracy charges in Georgia. The case was set for trial that October, but the key witness was nowhere to be found. Johnny Frank Stringfellow was a soldier who was serving a sentence in a federal prison for violating military code. He agreed to work as an undercover informant during the investigation of Davis, Revel and Allred in exchange for a lesser sentence. He wrote a letter to the federal agents who were investigating the liquor case, but unfortunately, it fell into the hands of some other criminals in Phenix City before it could be mailed.

The information reached the three Phenix City hoods, and they agreed that something needed to be done in order to stop Stringfellow from testifying about what he knew. Joe Allred knew someone who had once been a friend of Stringfellow's. His name was Wilson McVeigh. McVeigh and his friend and work colleague, Dave Walden, worked in the shipyards in Brunswick, Georgia, but spent their weekends in Phenix City stealing what they could and cracking safes for dope money to support their morphine habits.

Shortly after the arrests of Davis, Revel and Allred, Wilson McVeigh and Dave Walden came into Godwin Davis's Manhattan Club in Phenix City. Joe Allred joined the two men at their table and began to discuss their recent issue regarding Johnny Stringfellow. Joe told them, "Head Revel, Godwin Davis and I are in some trouble and might have to do time if the government witness testifies in federal court." "Who's putting the heat on you?" McVeigh asked. "A soldier who's gone undercover for the government named Johnny Frank Stringfellow," Allred replied. "Hell, I know him. He used to be a friend of mine," McVeigh said. Allred told McVeigh and Walden it would be worth something if they could help make Stringfellow disappear, and the hit men agreed, for the sum of $1,000, to carry out the assassination.

The agreement was that McVeigh and Walden would be paid once they delivered Stringfellow's body DOD (dead on delivery) to Head Revel at his summer home in St. Augustine, Florida. McVeigh was able to contact Stringfellow, and the ominous plot began to unfold. McVeigh invited Stringfellow to spend the weekend with him in Brunswick. After Wilson McVeigh and Dave Walden finished work at the shipyard, they went to Fitzgerald, Georgia, where McVeigh and his wife lived. At McVeigh's home, they began heating up morphine and shooting up to get high. Stringfellow asked for a hit, and McVeigh loaded up a lethal dose and gave it to him. As soon as the deadly poison hit his veins, Johnny collapsed and died.

McVeigh and Walden had killed Stringfellow, but now they needed to make the trip to Florida to show Head Revel that he was dead in order to get paid. They waited an hour and a half to make sure Johnny was dead. Then they got a drinking glass and held it over his mouth to see if there was any sign of life left in him. All indications were that Johnny was indeed dead, but McVeigh and Walden were in a state of drug-induced paranoia. If by chance he wasn't dead and came to, they would run the risk of being caught or, worse, not following through with the deal they had made with the Phenix City thugs.

The two hit men rolled Johnny's lifeless body into an old army blanket, placed him in the backseat of their car and headed for the Florida state line. Just outside town, McVeigh's paranoia made him think he heard Johnny moaning in the back of the car. He shouted for Walden to pull over, and McVeigh loaded up another lethal dose of morphine and punched it into Johnny's lifeless arm. They drove for several hours until they reached Ponte Vedre, which was about ten miles from Revel's home in St. Augustine. They pulled into a swampy, wooded area and took Johnny's corpse from the backseat. Still paranoid and confused, McVeigh held a .22 pistol to Stringfellow's head but couldn't pull the trigger. He remembered that at one time the two had been friends, and while in his emotional state of confusion, Walden grabbed the gun from him and pulled the trigger.

McVeigh and Walden covered the body and took off into town to find Head Revel. Revel and the two hit men went back out to where Johnny's body was hidden in the palmetto grove. He was satisfied that Stringfellow was dead and ordered them to dig a grave while he went back into town for a bag of lime to cover the body. When he returned, McVeigh and Walden had dug a shallow grave, just a few feet deep, and stripped Johnny of his clothes, except for his shoes. They covered the body in lime and dirt, and then McVeigh turned to Revel and said, "There's your man. Dead on delivery."

He ain't never gonna testify against nobody." Revel then took out a wad of cash from his pocket and paid the men for the deadly deed.

Sometime after the Stringfellow murder, Walden and McVeigh would be involved in another crime, but this time, it was even more personal. Dave Walden had married a girl from Columbus, Georgia, named Patricia Ann Archer. She was a beautiful dark-haired woman with two small children from a previous marriage. She hadn't been married to Dave Walden a week when she discovered some documents and stacks of cash and began to question the legitimacy of his business outings in Phenix City. She confronted Dave and threatened to contact the police over the matter. It would be the last thing she ever did; Dave made sure of that.

An argument broke out between the couple while they were driving through town, and when Patricia saw a policeman standing in a nearby parking lot, she said, "I ought to get out of this car right now and tell that policeman everything I know." Just then, in a moment of terrifying silence, Dave Walden glanced in the rearview mirror at his friend Wilson McVeigh in the backseat. McVeigh violently crashed a soda bottle over Patricia's head, knocking her unconscious. They drove her out of town and choked

The Okefenokee Swamp, near the Georgia-Florida state line, was a common dumpsite for victims of murder. Several bodies of men and woman who died at the hands of Phenix City thugs and hit men were taken to the swamp and thrown in.

her to death with a siphon tube, then crushed her skull with a tire iron. Just as they'd done with Stringfellow, they drove Patricia's corpse into the Okefenokee Swamp on the Florida-Georgia line, stripped off her clothes and tossed her into the black, murky depths of the swamp.

Years later, both McVeigh and Walden were arrested on drug charges and sent to prison. In March 1948, the Columbus, Georgia sheriff, E.F. Howell, got a tip that led to the arrest of a man named Roy Williamson. Williamson was a criminal safe cracker from Memphis, Tennessee, and a petty thief, but he had shared a cell with McVeigh and Walden while in prison. He told the sheriff about the stories Walden and McVeigh told him, and Sheriff Howell had Walden brought in from jail in Florida and McVeigh from prison in Georgia. When the investigators questioned the two men, they both confessed to the murders of Johnny Frank Stringfellow and Patricia Ann Archer.

The bodies of both victims were recovered, and indictments for murder in the first degree were returned for Dave Walden, Wilson McVeigh, Head Revel, Godwin Davis and Joe Allred. Georgia law, at the time, required the testimony of only two witnesses against a third party, and McVeigh and Walden confessed. They went on to serve life in prison, but the charges against the Dixie mafia boys from Phenix City were dropped.

Shortly after being sent to prison, Walden escaped, and immediate notice was sent out to authorities to recover the convict. He stayed on the run for nearly a month until a Tallahassee, Florida policeman spotted him. He was sitting under a shade tree next to a pond with a case of whiskey and about $4,000 cash that he had taken in a recent store robbery. He was drunk when the policeman arrested him, confessing to his escape and giving the details of how he sawed his way out of his cell with a smuggled hacksaw. He claimed that Head Revel aided him in his escape, meeting him with a car and driving him out of town. Walden went on, "I'm the best safe ripper in this part of the country, and you'd of never caught me if I hadn't gone and gotten drunk on that case of whiskey."

Safe Cracking 101

Allied vices and the Dixie mafia syndicate had spread out all over Phenix City and Russell County during the 1950s. It was a place that was known for its criminal enterprises and for the kind of people who worked for and

Perhaps no other city in America offered an "education" in safe cracking except for Phenix City, Alabama. Criminals from other states came to Phenix City to learn how to properly crack, shred and bust open safes from the Phenix City mafia men who made it their area of expertise.

within the Phenix City machine. Pimps, prostitutes, dope pushers, hit men, crooked politicians, lawyers and law enforcement, along with every form of corrupt individual within general society, seemed to flock to Phenix City in order to experience sin or get paid for crimes that required some sort of criminal expertise.

This was the case for a small group of syndicate men who were known for their expert "safe cracking" abilities. A good safe cracker was able to use standard, everyday mechanic's tools and a good ear to break into a safe. Several different methods were used, from drilling a hole inside the combination lock to listening through a specially designed stethoscope for the pops inside the gear door that would indicate the correct combination. Tools like saws, homemade pop locks, crow bars, sledge hammers and electric drills were used to pop and smash open safes in order to take the valuable contents that were hidden inside.

Perhaps no other city in the world offered an "education" in safe cracking except for Phenix City, Alabama. Syndicate member and gambler Head Revel was known for his involvement in criminal activity during the Sin City era. Members of Revel's band of safe crackers were assigned missions according to the highest bidder. He supplied information about the locations of loaded safes to local hoods in exchange for their services, and the loot was split up accordingly.

James Bush was one of those hoods and was considered the clown of the Phenix City mafia. He was a family man and always a card, pulling pranks and cracking jokes when he wasn't cracking safes. Before he became involved in Revel's school for safe cracking, he spent a lot of time pulling low-profile heists and climbing to the top of the Manhattan Club on Fourteenth Street to shoot soldiers in the rear with an air rifle for fun. This act of fun didn't go well for him on one occasion when he popped a pellet in the thigh of a paratrooper, who caught sight of him and stormed to the top of the club for a fight. When the soldier reached Bush, they fought for several minutes, trading blow for blow until the hefty trooper knocked him down. Bush grabbed a stray brick and went to bust the soldier in the head when it slipped and crashed through the skylight of the club's poker room.

Hawk Howard was a Phenix City card shark and gambler but was also known for his stone-cold poker face and his no-nonsense personality. He was grazed by the brick that came through the skylight when it smashed onto the card table where he was dealing. Hawk gracefully reached for his pistol and, without hesitation, unloaded it into the broken window, forcing Bush and the paratrooper to jump from the building to safety. Bush was also known for his witty scams that outsmarted some of the area's best card players. He once helped his associate defeat Blink Roberts in a game of poker by tying a string from his foot to his partner's pants leg. As Bush watched the game from a position that enabled him to see Blink's cards, he was able to signal his friend by pulling the string, cheating Blink out of the game.

James Bush was also one of Revel's bandits who ran a local club called the Spider Web. Bush employed a young man who was nineteen at the time and had recently been in trouble for his part in a rash of thefts. Lester Davis, who swore out the warrant against Bush's young apprentice for attempted auto theft, was walking to his car on the night of May 5, 1950, when he was confronted by a speeding car that opened fire on him. Bush and his sidekick chased Lester Davis through the streets of Phenix City at eighty miles per hour, terrorizing residents as stray bullets flew through their neighborhoods. Bush and his accomplice were later arrested for assault and attempted murder.

Johnny Benefield was another one of Revel's best safe crackers. He was known in Alabama, Georgia, Mississippi, Florida and even Tennessee for his expertise in busting bank safes. Once he was involved in Revel's outfit, they spent a good bit of time organizing heists. They scoped out potential high-rolling businesses for safes full of cash, drew up plans for breaking in and made sure every course of action was diligently organized.

Benefield was very successful at his trade, and he didn't teach his skill to outsiders—making him a very valuable asset to Revel. Benefield's techniques for breaking into safes varied. He was able to bore a hole next to the combination lock and look inside with a small head lamp and watch for the gears to fall. This required him to have well-trained eyes and ears, and he studied in a barn that was located across the street from Joe Allred's gas station, which was located on Highway 80 in Russell County. At Allred's barn, they also manufactured safe-cracking tools and would occasionally bring stolen safes there to crack.

Besides the tools of the trade, a few hot rods were needed in order to get the heisters away from the law as quickly as possible. Johnny Benefield owned several; one was a 1950s model Hudson. Johnny claimed he bought the Hudson hotrod from an African American man named Charlie Little. Little got the car from a man named Robert Johnson, who was doing time in a Georgia prison. Johnson was incarcerated for his part in a safe-cracking job in Fitzgerald, Georgia, on Halloween night in 1953. Over $223,000 in cash money and jewels were stolen from the store in Fitzgerald, which also found its way back to Head Revel. Those large sums of money and valuables were the main source of financing for Revel's lottery business.

Johnny Benefield and the rest of his safe cracking cronies were arrested and charged for the crimes they committed in Phenix City during the cleanup of 1954. His burglary tools, getaway cars and colleagues were all taken down in one of the nation's most infamous military operations.

Men Among Men

The syndicates and slums of Phenix City had ruled the town with an iron fist for decades by 1954. From the inside out, Phenix City was corrupt—from the general population to the highest-ranking city officials. Men like Hugh Bentley and Albert Patterson had watched the city's villains control every aspect, from voter fraud to tax evasion and murder. Not to mention the daily grind of gambling, lottery and liquor. The cries and pleas of Phenix City's citizens were heard. Together, Bentley and Patterson would work to stop the iniquitous and unlawful circumstances that were taking over the little city by the river and formed an organization called the Russell County Betterment Association (RBA) in order to help take down the Dixie mafia and rid the town of crime and vice once and for all.

Teaming up with church groups, anti-saloon leagues, women's auxiliaries and fed-up citizens, they forged a fight against that machine that would result in all-out war. When the average citizen or abused soldier stood up to the gamblers, dope pushers and pimps of Phenix City, a fight usually followed, but no one could prepare themselves for the circumstances that would follow the rising up of an entire town. The bloodshed had to be stopped. Children were being taught by policemen how to gamble their milk and paper route money. The city's youth were turning into the next generation of hoods; their school papers showed a direct correlation when students declared, "When I grow up, I want to run a gambling house." The city was falling apart at the seams, and something had to be done in order to stop it. Phenix City would be idle no more.

Hugh Bentley

Hugh Bentley was a Phenix City native who had grown up in the gambling communities of Russell County. His father ran a gambling house that essentially led to the separation and divorce of his parents. Hugh was born in 1909, and one of his first memories was standing next to his mother when he was no older than three or four as she preached about the sin of gambling to his father. Her pleas and influence fell on the deaf ears of Calvin Bentley, and a few years later, she packed up her seven boys and left. Minnie Bentley made the best living she could for her children, working as a cook for millworkers and as a seamstress. She preached the gospel to her boys in the hopes they would grow up with good morals and be deterred from the hell that festered in the tiny community of Girard in Phenix City.

Huge grew up and was ambitious. He studied the Bible and ran a sporting goods store, where he did very well for himself and his family. One of Hugh's first experiences with the violence in Phenix City sparked a fire in him that would not subside. When Bentley attended a sporting goods convention in Chicago, a fellow attendee laughed hysterically at Bentley when he told him he was from Phenix City. The man explained to Hugh that when he was in the army, he was stationed at Fort Benning, and he knew about the gambling, liquor and sex that existed in the city. Bentley took this as a major insult, not believing that the bars and clubs were as bad as this man made them out to be. Bentley was a man of God. He taught Sunday school at his church, and when the church bells chimed on Sunday mornings, all of his community was in attendance, including many of the local gangsters and gamblers.

When Bentley returned home from the conference, he told his wife, Bernice, about the conversation he had in Chicago. She agreed that the city had always had drinking, gambling and occasional fights, but from their perspective, Phenix City wasn't that bad. Bentley and his friend Hugh Britton decided that they would take a trip into the red-light districts of Phenix City on a Saturday night, just to see if the horror stories of the slums were even remotely true.

As they drove down Fourteenth and Dillingham Streets, they couldn't help but see the endless stream of cars coming over the bridge from Columbus. Smoke bellowed from the open doors of crowded cafés, and catcalls and applause roared from inside the strip clubs. The smell of liquor and stale beer was so pungent, you could almost get drunk just walking down the sidewalk. Neon signs flashed, "GIRLS! GIRLS! GIRLS!" while curvy females dressed in short, thigh-high skirts with low-cut tops hung outside the clubs asking the passing soldiers, "Buy me a drink, honey?" The cafés and clubs were lit up like lighthouses, bringing in ships of soldiers from across the Chattahoochee River. The whizzing sound of roulette wheels buzzed like a hive of angry bees as gamblers in their fancy suits and cigars drove up in fine automobiles, tossing over the keys to the car park and confidently strutting inside for a night of money, women and drunken debauchery.

When Bentley and Britton decided to go inside the clubs, they watched as soldiers were taken advantage of by B-girls and shifty bartenders poured half-drunk shots of whiskey back into bottles. Inside one of the local strip joints, they were met by a hefty bouncer who wouldn't allow them to enter. As Bentley argued with the doorman, Britton peered inside and saw several naked ladies dressed in nothing but lacy garters dancing around a horseshoe-shaped stage taking money from a slew of soldiers. When Bentley and Britton tried to cross the threshold of the club, the bouncer pushed the two men outside and told them, "You make one more move, feller, and I'll tear your head off and hand it to you." Fearing that trouble was coming, they decided it was in their best interest to go home.

As they went to the car, they discussed how awful it was that the truth about the city was right under their noses and had been for a long time. As they got into the car, the sound of heavy fist blows and grunts came from a nearby alley. They looked and saw three large men relentlessly beating the hell out of a young soldier. When Bentley tried to intervene, one of the men said, "You wanna be next?" Britton and Bentley rushed to the sheriff's department to report the fight. When they approached Sheriff Matthews, he told them to mind their own business and said it wasn't his jurisdiction to handle the affair. They then turned to the police chief for help. He told them he didn't have the manpower to spare. Bentley called the Fort Benning Military Police to report the incident, and they assured him that someone would be out to check on the situation in Shirttail Alley.

After several failed attempts to get the police and even Mayor Cobb involved in investigating the fight, Bentley and Britton gave up on the matter and went home just before dawn. The following morning, after church, the two men drove back into the city slums for another look at the place. Instead of parking in the alley, they parked just near the Dillingham Street Bridge, shut off the car and got out. As they began to walk down the sidewalk, they heard groans and sighs of agony coming from a clump of kudzu vines just at the bank of the river. Bentley looked over in the shrubbery and saw a young soldier of about eighteen curled up in the fetal position, clutching his abdomen in pain. The men slowly flipped him over and found that his face had been ripped to shreds. Britton and Bentley slowly lifted the beaten soldier, placed him in the backseat of their car and quickly sped off to Fort Benning.

Bentley tried to reassure the soldier that he was going to be OK, but the soldier insisted he couldn't go to the base. Whoever had mugged him had also taken his boots. "My sergeant will bust my ass for losing my boots," he said. Bentley, trying desperately to console the young man, told him not to worry about the boots and asked the soldier what had happened. "They promised us a private show," he said. "Then, when they closed the club, they came after us with spiked brass knuckles, clubs and chained fists. They took all my money and my boots. They took my boots!" When the car stopped at Martin Army Hospital at Fort Benning, they unloaded the young man and gave a report to the military police about what they'd seen and how they'd found the soldier by the river. The terrible reality was now evident, and Hugh Bently knew this wouldn't be the last experience they would have with the Phenix City syndicate groups.

After Bentley's investigation of Phenix City's club districts, he decided that it would be his personal war to clean up the city. Britton backed his every move, and from their first experience with the slums and red-light districts, Hugh Bentley refused to back down from any of Phenix City's gangsters. He organized a group of concerned citizens and church and auxiliary groups to form the RBA, Russell County Betterment Association. Their main goal was to eradicate the vice districts of Phenix City and run the gamblers, dope pushers, prostitutes and bootleggers out of town. But it wasn't that easy. Hoyt Shepherd had swayed from his gambling roots in an effort to gain another foot hold in the city as a financial backer for politicians. He may have been on the outside of gambling, but he kept the corruption of the city under lock and key with his means of buying out voters, covering up voter fraud and intimidating citizens during city elections.

When the Phenix City mob was on the inside with city officials, everyone from police, deputies, lawyers, politicians and even the mayor could be bought or bribed under some financial arrangement. There was no price too high for any political candidate who needed mafia assistance. Security, elected officials and tight lips kept the state agents from finding any wrong-doing in Phenix City, and the problem progressed for several years until it reached a critical stage for Bentley and the RBA. When the RBA intervened or spoke out against the crooked elections and bad business that was happening in Russell County, threats and intimidation tactics were used to scare people from joining or supporting the RBA. But those smokescreen tactics would change dramatically on January 9, 1952.

That morning, Hugh Bentley reluctantly traveled to Augusta, Georgia, with his brother to take him to the Veterans Hospital. Since Hugh's involvement in the RBA, he was getting repeated death threats from anonymous callers, and he was very apprehensive about leaving his wife and children at home.

Sometime just after midnight, Hugh pulled into his driveway from his long journey and found his home in ruins. The whole house had collapsed, and the dust from the recent catastrophe hadn't even settled when he sped his car into the driveway and dove from the driver's door, scrambling into the rubble to find his family.

As Hugh sifted through the debris, he could hear the faint voice of his eldest son, Hughbo. When Hugh found him alive, he was moved to tears and asked his son what happened. Hughbo explained that he didn't know. He was sleeping, and there was a loud explosion; he found himself outside on the ground. Hugh gathered his son and went toward the middle of the house searching for his wife; their young son, Thurman; and his nephew Mike. Hugh found Bernice and Truman together. Both were alive but very battered by the explosion. Hughbo also found Mike, and the ultimate miracle of the entire family found alive brought Hugh Bentley to his knees.

He gathered his family around him and wept as he prayed: "Thank you, dear Lord, for sparing my family the harm that was intended in this act of violence. I accept it as a sign to continue to work diligently to do your work to rid our town and our people of the evil that threatens us and surrounds us. Amen." Hearing about the attack, Hugh Britton was the first to arrive,

In January 1952, the Dixie mafia attempted to assassinate RBA member Hugh Bentley and his family. Miraculously, the entire family escaped with few injuries.

followed by the sheriff, Ralph Matthews. Matthews naïvely asked if Bentley's oil heater had blown up. Bentley barked back at him that he knew very well what had happened and demanded an investigation by the state to arrest the culprit who cowardly attempted to murder his family.

Demolition specialists from Fort Benning came and took part in the investigation of the bombing of Hugh Bentley's home. They determined that the cause was dynamite, which had been placed under Bentley's porch. They added that this was most likely done by an amateur with some knowledge of how explosives work. A reward was issued that reached almost $9,000 for information pertaining to the Bentley bombing, but few leads came back during the investigation. Later, some incriminating evidence came out during a trial that would indicate that a local thug known as Tommy "Dynamite" Capps was allegedly responsible for the bombing under order from or in association with Deputy Albert Fuller.

Tommy Capps was one of a few go-to guys when the dirty work needed to be handled. According to witness reports, Tommy Capps was also known for his brutality toward women. He was a bouncer at the Hill-Top House bordello, which was one of Phenix City's most depraved whorehouses. It was dirty and unkempt, with drug-addicted woman who worked in the sex trade for whatever price offered. Dynamite was also called on by city officials on occasion. It was noted that he was frequently seen at the courthouse in Russell County speaking to the sheriff and other syndicate-elected officials like Solicitor Arch Ferrell, who was operating behind the scenes for the Phenix City machine.

Ferrell's part in the syndicate was relatively simple. As the district attorney, he had the power to indict or let go anyone who was arrested by the already corrupt law enforcement in Russell County and Phenix City. He was known for his explosive temper and equally explosive behavior when he drank too much. During a town rally for the Bentleys, in response to their home being bombed and to address the community about the crime that existed in the city, Arch Ferrell and several other syndicate members were called out for their part in the corruption, creating a firestorm that would drive the citizens of Phenix City to back the RBA and finally expose the gangsters for what they were.

One by one, each of the syndicate members stood up in defiance of the media reports and accusations that Phenix City was a den of sin and haven for crooks. The crooked city officials assured the citizens that Phenix City was a clean and law-abiding town. When a man stood up from his seat and shouted at Ferrell, "Liar!" Ferrell's sister Eugenia shouted back at him,

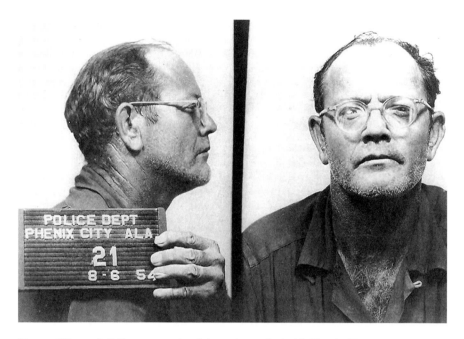

Tommy "Dynamite" Capps was a local thug who worked with Phenix City gangsters and other criminal organizations. He was allegedly responsible for the bombing of Hugh Bentley's home in 1952. However, Capps was never formally charged for the attempted murder of the Bentley family, and no arrest were ever made.

"Don't you call my brother a liar!" The man again shouted at Ferrell, and at that point Eugenia lunged toward the man and slapped him across the face. Arch Ferrell followed by leaping from the stage and running toward the man, but he was restrained by Sheriff Matthews and another state patrolman. As Ferrell was being held back, he told the man if he had something to get off his chest, they could take it outside, and the patrolman then directed the man who'd been slapped to leave.

The RBA began to make threats of its own, telling the community that impeachment of the city officials would be the next step in order to bring down the internal corruption in the judicial system. Ferrell fired back at the RBA and told its members he dared them to try to impeach him, calling out the secret attorney who had been advising the RBA. Someone called out from the crowd that the RBA lawyer was a good one, and Ferrell replied, "I know he is, and I'm ready to face him in any impeachment proceedings."

As the unrest of the community and the Bentley bombing investigation progressed, little information was turned up in order to make an arrest and bring the culprit to justice. The community was growing uneasy, and the violence escalated to a point where no one felt safe. The honky-tonks and juke joints were still blasting away in Phenix City, as its citizens lived in terror, walking their children to school and never letting them out of their sight for very long. Under circumstances in which a good Christian man like Hugh Bentley could be attacked in an effort to harm or kill his wife and children, the rest of the community was concerned about its support of Bentley and the RBA. It was an ugly but true reality. Like all chaotic situations, things would get worse—much worse—before they got better.

Albert Patterson

Albert Patterson was born in Tallapoosa County, Alabama, in 1894, not far from the location of the infamous Indian Wars at Horseshoe Bend. His family depended on farming to make a living, and when he was just shy of manhood, he left Alabama to work in the Texas oil fields. In 1916, when he was twenty-two, Patterson enlisted in the United States Army with the Third Texas Infantry, and in 1917, he married Agnes Benson, with whom he'd fallen in love while on leave in Alabama. In 1918, Albert Patterson was shipped to France to fight in the First World War. While fighting, he sustained a substantial injury to his right leg that ended his military career and forced him to walk with the aid of a cane for the rest of his life.

When Albert Patterson returned to Alabama, he was able to get a job as a teacher and worked in the school system for several years. Along the way, he put himself through school in order to further his education. He graduated from the University of Alabama in 1924 with a bachelor's degree in history. In 1926, he continued to pursue his legal education and received his law degree from the Cumberland Law School in Lebanon, Tennessee. In 1927, he opened his first law practice in Opelika, Alabama, but relocated the following year to Alexander City. He finally settled in Phenix City in 1933, opening his law office in the Coulter Building.

Patterson knew about the city's activities and was no stranger to the crime lords and gangsters who ran it. On more than one occasion, he was hired to defend them, including mob kingpin Hoyt Shepherd and several others. Patterson's involvement with the city as an attorney was a double-edged sword. He was sworn to uphold the law and defend those who needed representation, but he was also bound and held down by the corruption of the city. Patterson was quiet in his efforts to strengthen the

Albert Patterson was a lawyer in Phenix City who joined forces with the RBA in an effort to clean up the town. He ran for attorney general in 1954 but was assassinated by members of syndicate groups before he could take office.

community for some time. He, like Hugh Bentley, was forced to watch as criminals went free at the hands of shady judges and irresponsible lawmen.

Patterson teamed up with Hugh Bentley and the RBA when Phenix City syndicates were at their most violent and malicious, and he was not immune to the retaliation from the mob. On February 24, 1952, he received a phone call that his office building was on fire. Someone had climbed onto the second-story roof and entered the building through a window. The intruder soaked the office with motor oil and set it on fire. Fortunately, the janitor caught the fire before it destroyed the building completely.

Once the police and sheriff arrived, they started an immediate investigation. However, no evidence of the arsonist's identity was ever found, and no arrest in the case were ever made. The *Columbus Ledger* covered the story and blatantly attacked the cowardly act that everyone knew had to do with the mob in Phenix City. Patterson was also receiving death threats, and he knew in his heart that he might not make it through the battle to save Phenix City.

Patterson, Bentley and the RBA agreed it was time to change their strategy and decided it would be best to try to vote out the corruption in Phenix City in the May elections. City and county officials had long been the syndicate's greatest source of control, and the machine had been backing its handpicked candidates since 1946, controlling every aspect of city and county government along the way. The recent attacks on Bentley and Patterson showed the citizens of Phenix City that if they didn't vote out those who sought to abuse and take advantage of the system, no one would be safe from the tyranny of the machine.

The first part of the RBA's plan was to get the mayor to ban all the registered gamblers from monitoring the polls during election. It then contacted the governor of Alabama and insisted that the state provide adequate supervision during voting in Phenix City in order to keep the gangsters from manipulating the polls and to stop them from intimidating the voters who came. That March, an editorial was printed in the *Columbus Ledger* that mentioned large amounts of money being donated to certain Phenix City groups and citizens. It also said that the presence of machine members and their election officers could be expected during the election. This was a good indication for the general public, as well as members of the RBA, that there was going to be some serious trouble on voting day.

On the morning of the elections, voters came down to the Fifth Avenue polls to cast their votes. Hugh Bentley and his son, along with Hugh Britton, went down to the polls and saw the same thing they had seen during every other city election. Gangsters were purchasing votes from poor millworkers for one dollar; pre-marked ballots, tombstone ballots and carloads of unqualified voters and prostitutes were being dropped off as they shouted back at the driver, "What name do I put on the ballot again?" It was a horrible and deceitful mess. Hugh Bentley went to Judge Harry Randall for help and demanded that the gangsters and fraudulent voters be arrested, but he refused.

When they went back down to the voting polls, they found Head Revel and several of his cronies blocking the booths. When Bentley confronted him and pushed through the line of oversized men to address the press, one of the gangsters grabbed Britton by his arm and spun him around, ripping off his sleeve as he swung at him with a sledge hammer. The blow sent Britton into a glass window, smashing it open and cutting Britton. The mob then attacked Bentley and his son. Bentley had spent some time as an amateur boxer in his teenage years, and he could hold his own, trading blow for blow with the bullies. The press from the *Ledger* quickly began to snap photos of the attack, and even Bentley's mother-in-law tried to intervene. She had been watching the polls and confronted a policeman, who said, "Lady, they're not going to hurt them. They're using their fists and feet."

Once the beating was over, Bentley, Britton and young Hughbo were taken to Cobb Hospital, where they were treated for their wounds and released. A couple of the thugs were arrested but later released and fined a

During the 1954 election in Phenix City, legitimate voters attempted to break through the lines of thugs blocking the polls. The thugs attacked them, and a violent fistfight followed, sending RBA member Hugh Britton through a plate glass window and injuring Hugh Bentley and his sixteen-year-old son.

small fee. The photos of the assault made national news, and suddenly the entire world knew of the violence and mayhem that existed in Phenix City, Alabama. It wouldn't be Alabama's dirty little secret anymore. No longer was the devil able to hide out in Phenix City. Once the mob was exposed for what it was, its days were numbered.

In 1954, Albert Patterson ran for attorney general against MacDonald Gallion, a lawyer from Montgomery, and Lee "Red" Porter, also an attorney from Gadsden. Known syndicate member and district attorney Arch Ferrell and the current attorney general, Silas Garrett, already had their chips on Porter, and he was handpicked by the machine to win the election. The threat of Albert Patterson winning the election for attorney general was very real to the machine, so it fired up the rumor wagon and began to slander and spread lies all over the city in an effort to discredit Patterson and discourage his supporters. Rumors of Patterson's involvement with the machine were backed by his previous involvement as an attorney for both Hoyt Shepherd and Head Revel in the murders of Fate Leebern and Johnny Stringfellow.

Rumors didn't stop Patterson. He turned over his law office and practice to his son, John, and began his campaign across the state. He spoke out about the tyranny of the gangs that had been running Phenix City into the ground. He addressed the issues of this behavior spreading throughout the state if it could not be stopped, and he pleaded with the people of Alabama to help him end the corruption. On June 10, 1954, the votes were counted, and despite the machine's best efforts to rig the election, Patterson won by 854 votes. The victory, however, was short lived. Immediately, syndicate members began to go to work intimidating and pressuring election officials over the outcome, calling for a recount.

Since Patterson's involvement with the RBA and his announcement to run for attorney general, the death threats continued and became more and more consistent. He told a group of RBA members during a church meeting after his win for attorney general that the chances of him making it to office were one hundred to one. He knew in his heart that this was the altar on which the sacrificial lamb would be placed, and on June 18, 1954, the blood of that lamb was spilled.

Patterson was working late that night but left his office at about 9:00 p.m. As he exited the building, approaching his car that was parked in the alley between the Coulter building and the Elite Café, an assailant approached him and shoved a pistol in his mouth. Without hesitation, the killer fired, shooting Patterson once in the mouth, once in the arm and again in the chest. Albert Patterson fell to the ground bleeding and mortally wounded. He died just minutes after the shooting.

A few minutes later, the district attorney, Arch Ferrell, and deputy, Albert Fuller, frantically entered the bathroom inside Dixie's Jones on Fourteenth Street. A soldier who was inside the stall overheard the two men: "I told you not to shoot him there, you sonofabitch!" Not knowing what was happening, the soldier played drunk and stumbled from the stall. He was able to get out of the bathroom unharmed. Shortly after, crowds of people were gathering in the alley where Patterson was murdered. News of his assassination flew over the media telephone lines until they reached the governor in Montgomery.

General "Crack" Hanna and Martial Law

As soon as the message regarding the assassination of Albert Patterson reached the state capital in Montgomery on the night of the murder, Governor Persons immediately contacted General Walter J. Hanna. Hanna was a Birmingham, Alabama native who had the heart and soul of a warrior. Hanna was fifteen the first time he went down to the army recruiter's office to enlist. When the recruiter found out how old he was, he immediately sent him on his way, telling him to stay in school. When Walter's father found out, he sat him down and talked with him about the importance of his education. Walter's older brother was already serving overseas in World War I, and the only thing he could think about was serving his country the same way. His father forbid him from going back down to the army station again, and Walter understood, but he tried several more times, even traveling outside Birmingham to other cities in an effort to get signed up.

He visited a marine recruiter one afternoon and spoke with a heavy-set, dog-faced sergeant about signing up. The marine sergeant didn't entertain the talk for very long when he found out how old Walter was. The angry recruiter shouted at Walter to get out and stop wasting his time. Frustrated and perhaps a little resentful, the little redheaded whippersnapper puffed up at the marine and took a swing. The marine sergeant easily avoided the punch, then grabbed Walter and flung him down the stairs. "Even the Salvation Army wouldn't take you!" he shouted as he slammed the door.

Disappointed and scuffed up, Walter Hanna held his head up and headed back to Birmingham, where he was finally successful in joining the Army

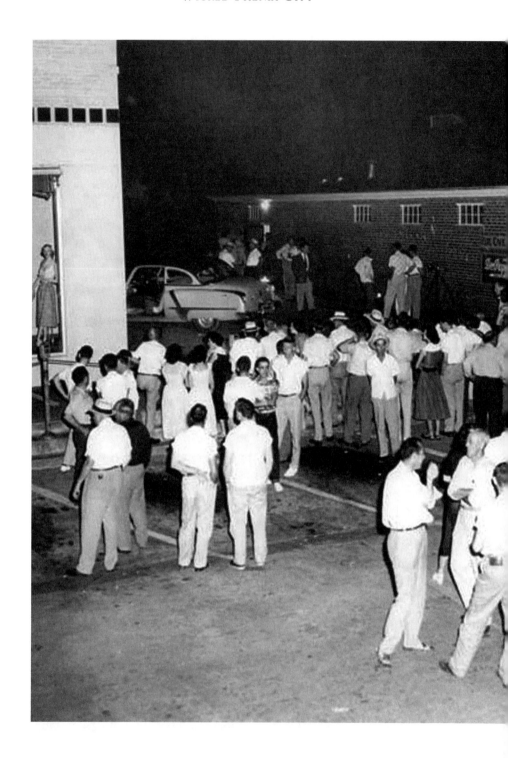

National Guard. When he finally built up the courage to tell his father, his reaction was harsh: "You know I ought to horsewhip you, Walter. You disobeyed my explicit order." "Yes, sir," Walter said, "but I felt like I had to do it." Walter's father knew he was tough enough to handle being in the army, regardless of his age. Though he wasn't happy with the way Walter went about it, he was still very proud of his son for his determination and desire to serve his country.

Walter was nineteen years old when men started returning from World War I, but he served his country well during World War II when he finally got his chance to go to war. He was skilled in combat, earning a reputation as a warrior. During heavy fighting in the jungles of Morotai, his unit was credited for over eighty enemy kills. He was also severely injured during a Japanese bombing, which crushed two of his vertebrate, shattered his knees and broke his

On June 18, 1954, Albert Patterson was assassinated outside his law office in the alley between the Coulter building and the Elite Cafe. He was shot once in the mouth, once in the arm and again in the chest.

nose. He insisted, even under such substantial injury, that the field surgeons bandage him up and let him get back to fighting.

This was the man who was chosen by Governor Persons to defend the citizens of Phenix City from the mob. Hanna left Birmingham on the night of the murder and made it to Phenix City in record time. As he reached the crime scene and stepped out of his Lincoln, he approached the alley where Patterson was murdered. Dozens of spectators and citizens were gathered around the location, milling about and whispering to one another as General Hanna approached the crowd. His cold stare was fixed on the misconduct of the murder scene: no police line, no deputies or investigators and contamination by dozens of people just loitering around.

General Hanna visited Cobb Hospital that night and spoke briefly with Patterson's widow and son, John. Hugh Bentley and members of the RBA were utterly devastated by Patterson's murder, and a heavy anxiety and sadness lingered over them all. General Hanna also went down to the gambling districts of Phenix City that night and was approaching the BAMA club when he heard what he thought were slot machines inside. J.D. Abney, who was the club operator at the time, flung the door open at Hanna and confronted the general head on. After some cross words and some threats, the general fired back at the crooks, saying, "The party's over. There will be no more gambling. Try it and I'll put you under the jail."

On June 19, 1954, national guardsmen from Alabama descended on Phenix City to keep the peace and protect the citizens. The first order of business for General Hanna was to investigate the claims of illegal activity that had been going on in the city for many years. Of course, the corrupt members of local law enforcement did their best to tip off the local gamblers and illegal establishments. Under the cover of night, truckloads of gambling equipment left the city, and some of the most notorious syndicate members were leaving town as well.

After Governor Persons met with the United States president Dwight Eisenhower and FBI chief J. Edgar Hoover in Washington, D.C., he called General Hanna for a meeting to explain the details. On July 22, 1952, Governor Persons tossed a copy of the proclamation across his desk to General Hanna and explained that at 4:30 p.m. he would be reading the orders to impose martial rule over Phenix City. The difference between martial rule and martial law is that under the rule, all law enforcement agencies will be terminated and replaced with military personnel until a time when a region can reestablish its local government. This was what General Hanna needed in order to get the job done. He went to Fort

Right: J. Edgar Hoover was the founder and first director of the Federal Bureau of Investigation. He also helped organize the secret police in Washington. Alabama governor Gordon Persons met with United States president Dwight D. Eisenhower and Hoover to discuss the criminal activity in Phenix City.

Below: On July 22, 1952, Governor Persons handed a copy of the proclamation to enforce martial rule in Phenix City to General Hanna. At approximately 4:30 p.m., the law was enforced, and fifteen thousand national guardsmen from Fort McClellan arrived in Phenix City.

McClellan that afternoon, gathered fifteen thousand troops and bussed them to Phenix City.

Instructing his men on the details of their mission, General Hanna explained that they were to dismantle the local government, starting with city hall and the courthouse in Russell County. They would then relieve all local law enforcement of their duties and protect the citizens. Hanna and his men

After martial rule was proclaimed in Phenix City, General Hanna's first order of business was to dismantle the local government in Russell County. Starting with city hall and the courthouse, Hanna and his men marched into the sheriff's office and fired Sheriff Matthews and his deputies. They then moved on to the Phenix City Police Department and did the same.

marched right into the Sheriff's Department and fired Sheriff Matthews and his deputies and then did the same at police headquarters. Martial rule existed for six months in Phenix City, and investigations turned up over twenty-eight murders with no indictments or convictions. The gamblers and syndicate members of the Phenix City underworld were systematically taken down and arrested for their crimes.

As for the murder of Albert Patterson, his alleged murderer, Albert Fuller, was sentenced to life in prison but was paroled after serving only ten years. Of Fuller's accomplices, Arch Ferrell, the fiery-tempered corrupt district attorney, was acquitted, and Silas Garret, the attorney general, was committed to a mental institution shortly after he was arrested for his part in the voter fraud and intimidation of officials during Patterson's election. Given the circumstances and the horrible nature of the crime, this didn't seem to bring justice to Phenix City. The grief-stricken community took many years to overcome the stigma that was left by these events.

Far better is it to dare mighty things, to win glorious triumphs, even though checkered by failure…than to rank with those poor spirits who neither enjoy nor suffer much, because they live in a gray twilight that knows not victory or defeat.
—*Theodore Roosevelt.*

Phenix Rising: The Rebirth of Phenix City

The crime lords, whorehouses, liquor joints and casinos of Phenix City were all shut down and removed. It took the death of Albert Patterson and the injustice of generations to accomplish the cleanup of Russell County and Phenix City. Nevertheless, order was restored, and John Patterson took up where his father left off, eventually running for governor of Alabama. When he was elected, he was the youngest governor in Alabama's history. Hugh Bentley continued his efforts working with the RBA, as did his colleagues, in order to keep the mob at bay. There were attempts by some syndicate members to regain strength in Phenix City, but the citizens and good people of Alabama would prevail and remain victorious.

It took several years for the people in Phenix City to recover from the tyranny and abuse that made it the Wickedest City in America. In 1955, the movie *The Phenix City Story* hit every theater in America, Mexico and parts of Europe. Suddenly, the entire world was introduced to the little Alabama town that had been riddled with vice and corruption throughout the 1940s and '50s. Many locals would often find it necessary to say they were from anywhere other than Phenix City, but others represented their hometown with pride.

Today, Phenix City is known for its hospitality and scenic beauty across the riverfront region. There is very little, if any, evidence of the honky-tonks and bars that once existed here. Occasionally, builders and renovators will stumble on hidden liquor cellars in the historic district homes. Some have even reported finding tunnels that lead out to the river, and often during draggings of the Chatthoochee River, cars, bodies and even loaded guns are found. The red-light districts of Phenix City have been erased from the landscape, and the mighty river has swallowed much of their forgotten history. The memory of those who survived these generations is still very fresh. The historical elements and details of just how bad Phenix City really was are often left to the history books and a handful of historians who still find it necessary to share those memories. They say time heals all wounds, and for the most part, this is probably true. The painful memory of a town that sprang up from Indian soil, built on slavery and nourished with crime, may be healed, but it will never be forgotten.

BIBLIOGRAPHY

Print

Atkins, Ace. *Wicked City*. New York: Berkley Books, 2008.

Barnes, Margaret Anne. *The Tragedy and the Triumph of Phenix City, Alabama*. Macon, GA: Mercer University Press, 1998.

Chapman, George. *Chief William McIntosh: A Man of Two Worlds*. Atlanta: Cherokee Publishing Company, 1988.

Cherry, F.L. *The History of Opelika and Her Agricultural Tributary Territory*. Opelika: Genealogical Society of East Alabama, 1996.

Grady, Alan. *When Good Men Do Nothing: The Assassination of Albert Patterson*. Tuscaloosa: University of Alabama Press, 1956.

Nunn, Alexander. *Lee County and Her Forebears*. Opelika, AL: published with the cooperation of Probate Judge Hal Smith and Commissioners J.G. Adams, Bobby J. Freeman, J.L. Hearn and Huey P. Long, n.d.

Serafin, Faith. *Haunted Columbus, Georgia: Phantoms of the Fountain City*. Charleston, SC: The History Press, Haunted America, 2012.

Strickland, Edwin, and Gene Wortman. *Phenix City Alabama: The Wickedest City in America*. Birmingham, AL: Vulcan Press, 1955.

Woolfolk, Elizabeth Carrow. *Pioneers, Patriots, and Planters*. Houston, TX: WCO Wynnton Publishing, 2004.

Interview

Sanders, Jim. Interviewed by author. March 28, 2014, Daviston, AL.

Websites

accessgenealogy.com
alabamapioneers.com
boards.ancestry.com
digital.library.okstate.edu
encyclopediaofalabama.org
files.usgwarchives.net
iml.jou.ufl.edu
lostworlds.org
phenixcityal.us
usacitiesonline.com

ABOUT THE AUTHOR

Faith Serafin is a historian and folklorist from southeast Alabama. She works as a full-time writer and photographer and is the official tour guide of the Sea Ghosts Tours at the National Civil War Naval Museum in Columbus, Georgia. Faith is also the host of Parafied–Overnight Ghost Hunts, and she is the founder and director of the Alabama Paranormal Research Team, a team of dedicated paranormal investigators and researchers. She also volunteers her time in local schools for reading workshops and creative writing classes. You can find out more about Faith's work by visting www.AlabamaGhostHunters.com.